Advance Praise for *Faith, Hope & Love*

In the new memoir *Faith, Hope & Love* by Jennifer France, the author tells of her communications with her deceased life partner, Ann Marie, in the three years following her death, as Jenn mourns her and grapples with the loss.

It is both heart-wrenching and compelling, as the story unfolds through Jenn's journal entries, "signs" she received from Ann Marie after taking her own life, and meetings with three psychic mediums. As they tell it, Ann Marie's desire to reach Jenn from the Other Side is strong—and there are some deeply heartfelt and humorous exchanges throughout. This leads to a better understanding of who Ann Marie was in life—an accomplished, loving person with many different sides to her—as well as Jenn's increased belief in the afterlife.

No matter whether you chalk such things up as hokum or, in the case of mediums, a shady sideshow, it is hard not to come away from the book with wonderment about the questions I think we all ponder at times: Where do we go after we no longer inhabit this earth? And if we could, would we reach out to a lost loved one to hopefully lessen our—and their—grief?

Faith, Hope & Love is billed as a memoir, but what it really is, is a love story. Jenn's personal experience led her to write the book. And it may make the skeptics out there into believers.

~ **Judith Pilone**

FAITH, HOPE & LOVE

FAITH, HOPE & LOVE

A Survivor's Memoir
Jennifer France

All rights reserved
First Edition—2024
Copyright © 2024—Jennifer France

No part of this book may be reproduced or transmitted in any form or by any means, electronic or mechanical, including photocopying, recording, or by any information storage and retrieval system, except as permitted by law.

For additional information, contact Jennifer France:
jennfrance.writes@gmail.com
https://www.jennfrancewrites.com

Permissions: See Permissions / Bibliography at the end.

ISBN Hardcover   979-8-9881089-0-0
ISBN Paperback   979-8-9881089-2-4
ISBN Ebook   979-8-9881089-1-7

Cover design by Pouneh France
Editing by Wendy C. Garfinkle (Grammar Goddess Editing)
Copy editing and proofreading by Julie Willson and Erika Steeves
Interior design by Susi Clark of Creative Blueprint Design

*This book is dedicated to Ann Marie Coppen and her infinite being.
I would like to also dedicate this song to her.*

"Evergreen" by Barbra Streisand

Love, soft as an easy chair
Love, fresh as the morning air
One love that is shared by two
I have found with you

Like a rose under the April snow
I was always certain love would grow
Love ageless and evergreen
Seldom seen by two

You and I will make each night a first
Every day a beginning
Spirits rise and their dance is unrehearsed
They warm and excite us
'Cause we have the brightest love

Two lights that shine as one
Morning glory and midnight sun
Time we've learned to sail above
Time won't change the meaning of one love
Ageless and ever—evergreen

Contents

Introduction 1

April 1, 2019: In The Beginning: The Purse 7

April 5, 2019: The First Song 11

"Just Breathe" (Live Version) by Pearl Jam 12

April 11, 2019: The Moth 15

April 13, 2019: Ann Marie Sighs 17

April 16, 2019: The First Dream 19

April 18, 2019: Rip The Band-Aid Off 23

April 25, 2019: The Letter That Wouldn't Stick 25

May 16, 2019: OUR HOME Pin On A Map 31

May 20, 2019: A Ladybug With Heart 33

May 27, 2019: Death By A Thousand Cuts 39

June 17, 2019: First Reading With Kay Fahlstrom,
    In Person, Sonoma, California 41

June 24, 2019: Grief Deepens You 53

June 25, 2019: First Reading With Sandra O'Hara,
    Via Skype 57

July 2, 2019: My Heart Still Hurts 63

"Everything I Own" by Bread 63

July 7, 2019: Breathing You In 67

"Incomplete" by James Bay 67

July 14, 2019: Second Reading With Kay Fahlstrom,
    Via Phone 71

July 20, 2019: She's Giving Me Strength Through Music 83

"Be Here Now" by Ray LaMontagne 83

August 8, 2019: She's In The Wind 85

August 20, 2019: Kindred Souls... 87

"This Ain't Goodbye" by Train 88

September 3, 2019: Second Reading With Jeanne Leto,
    Via Phone 91

October 5, 2019: Second Reading With Sandra O'Hara,
    In Person, Mill Valley, California..................... 107

October 6, 2019: Breathing Her In 119

"One More Kiss, Dear" by Vangelis 119

October 25, 2019: 3358 & March 27 125

November 9, 2019: Music Was My Best Friend.................. 127

"Afterglow" by Taylor Swift.. 128

December 15, 2019: Third Reading With Jeanne Leto,
    Via Phone 131

December 20, 2019: The Driveway Song 139

"All We Are" by Matt Nathanson................................. 140

December 24, 2019: Ann Marie's Ornaments 143

January 1, 2020: The Significance Of Numbers 147

    January 1, 2020: Journal Entry 148

    January 2, 2020: Journal Entry 148

    January 3, 2020: Journal Entry 149

    January 4, 2020: Journal Entry 150

    January 5, 2020: Journal Entry 150

March 24, 2020: A Double Rainbow 153

April 14, 2020: Fourth Reading With Jeanne Leto,
        Via Phone 157

April 21, 2020: Third Reading With Kay Fahlstrom,
        Via Phone 167

June 1, 2021: My Desktop Has A Mind Of Its Own 175

September 23, 2021: Darling, It's Me—One Last Song 177

    "Darling" by Halsey 178

January 16, 2022: Birthday Wishes 181

About The Author 183

Acknowledgments 185

Medium Biographies 187

    Jeanne Leto, Medium 187

    Kay Fahlstrom, Medium 188

    Sandra O'Hara, Medium 189

Permissions / Bibliography 191

Introduction

When I first started my journal, it was merely a way of keeping track of my daily activities after Ann Marie's passing. My mind was a jumbled mess of thoughts and emotions: questions … so many questions … confusion, guilt, fog, and loneliness. I struggled to make sense of what had happened. Every day was like walking through life wearing concrete shoes. And the nights were just as difficult. Mostly, I prayed.

I never once blamed Ann Marie; I never got angry with her. I waited for that feeling to arrive, but it never came, and I don't think it ever will. Confused, yes, but never angry.

After her passing, I almost immediately felt this overwhelming connection to God, the universe, Jesus (whatever word you like), something out there in charge and in control of everything, even Ann Marie's death. She'd made it a part of her life story to teach me that I had truly never had faith. I believed I did, but I was so wrong. That was Ann Marie's greatest gift to me. She sacrificed so my Soul could grow and expand. She was my savior.

I went to a Catholic school in my early childhood. Church on Wednesday at noon for all grades and time spent learning the Bible. My family did not attend church regularly, but we were brought up to believe in God, nonetheless. I was never a religious child or adult. Even as a young girl, maybe at the age of seven or eight, I felt there were too many inconsistencies surrounding religion. So at that point, I had decided that my spirituality would be on my terms.

Me and God. I believed in God. I believed that there was a God to talk to, but I never took Him up on that offer. Life wasn't perfect, but it was good. I was blessed and felt lucky to have so much of what others lacked. I had struggles and challenges as we all do, but never thought I could talk to God. In my small-minded human brain I thought, *I can't bother God with my problems. He has larger concerns at hand. People who have much larger problems than I do. Wars, famines, single moms raising children, people without homes or food.* I didn't want to waste His limited resources on me.

That is where I had it so wrong. God has no limitations. He is infinite and limitless, but I did not realize that until Ann Marie's death. Before this revelation, I rarely spoke to Him. I rarely asked for help, and I never asked for guidance. I wasn't walking hand in hand with Him. I was isolated and alone, believing I could do it all on my own. Boy, did I have it all wrong! The extreme heartbreak of Ann Marie's death taught me that. I had been broken wide open with nowhere to turn but God, Jesus, and the universe. Now I see that is all God wants for me, to share all my life with Him, good and bad. Share my joy and my sorrow. I realize now that is all He has ever wanted. His strength is limitless.

A month or so into journaling, I found that daily writing was my lifeline and one of many cornerstones to my healing. I waited for those private moments alone when I could sit in my writing space with photos of Ann Marie and me together and with our family, and with candles and soft piano music. I felt as if it was "our" time. When I could share with her how much I loved her. I wanted Ann Marie to know I could never be upset with her. I wanted her to hear my words and thoughts. I had made up my mind that I would form every letter as carefully and as slowly as I could, believing somehow that I was etching those words onto Ann Marie's Soul. I would faithfully remember as many details about her as I could. I didn't want to forget anything about her. I came to realize my journaling was a straight path of clear communication with Ann Marie and the universe.

I want to share my story, so Ann Marie is never forgotten. And to give, if only to one person, a sense of peace and faith that their loved one who has passed is still there, through their grief, and will always be there, albeit unseen and just beyond the veil, doing their best to communicate with you. In my humble opinion, I believe the degree of communication depends on many variables. The strength and determination of the one who has passed, and the openness and receptivity of the one remaining are two major factors.

Ann Marie was the most amazing human being I have ever met. Anyone who knew her would agree. I cannot tell you why she touched me so deeply, because she was not perfect by any stretch of the imagination, and she would readily admit to that. When I think about all she was, in the end, I think it was her vulnerability that bound me to her. She let me see all of her: the beautiful, the good, the bad, and the ugly. She was who she was.

Her sense of humor ... boy, did we laugh. Something about her tickled my funny bone, and she understood my dry, silly, dorkish humor. Sometimes she seemed like a grumpy old man, and even that was endearing. Her laughter was infectious. Once, while in San Francisco at a comedy club, the comedian we had gone to see commented onstage that he would love to have her at every show, sitting in the front row.

She was honest in all things; she spoke it how she saw it, even if it was way off base. I admired her for that. Her temper was rare but could be intimidating. Often, I would just listen, and then she would typically apologize for her poor behavior. I always accepted her apologies straightaway. Her intelligence … I can't even pinpoint it. Did she have a photographic memory or was she just off-the-charts smart? I don't know and suspect I never will. Her perseverance and determination … I've never known such a strong-willed human being. If something was to be done, she would get it done, and her work ethic was admirable. All I knew and cared about was I loved this woman to her core … and that will never change. She was vibrant and unique. Her outward beauty, to me, was unmatched. She was everything I had always desired in every physical way.

Most days, I felt like the luckiest person walking the face of the Earth. I was happy. Such a simple word, but when truly felt, it's life-altering. What made our love earth-shattering is that we felt it equally.

I would be remiss if I did not mention that I suspect Ann Marie was bipolar (she always refused to be tested for neurodivergence), and it made for some difficult times. It was not all sugar cakes and roses. We had plenty of bumps in the road.

My communications with Ann Marie and the Other Side began almost immediately. And thank goodness for my journal, because I could not have possibly remembered all the miracles that were to transpire over the next two and a half years and continue to transpire even today. In this book, I've shared a small portion of the many ways Ann Marie and I communicated with each other. I hope that what you read brings you some form of peace, knowing we all go somewhere, and it is not over when we move on from this realm. My experiences with the Other Side and Ann Marie have changed my life.

Ann Marie passed away sometime between the hours of 1 a.m. and 8 a.m. on March 27, 2019. I know this because we'd had an argument, I had left the house to stay in a hotel, and we were texting up until 1 a.m. I share custody of my twin daughters with my ex, and on this day, I was grateful they were with her. Ann Marie had five years with our children. She came into their lives when they were two years old, after my divorce was final. I do believe she knew they were away—which gave her free rein to do what she did. She was consistent about minding her manners when we had our children in our home.

I arrived home on the twenty-seventh, a Wednesday, at approximately 8:15 a.m. That is when I found Ann Marie dead by her own hand.

Jennifer France
San Carlos, California
August 2022

April 1, 2019

In The Beginning: The Purse

This was the date of Ann Marie's first communication with me, five days after her passing. On March 30, my sister and I gently packed Ann Marie's belongings to give to her family, who had flown in from Florida. I was in a daze, my mind trying to wrap around what was happening. I barely knew what I was doing. I was a body on autopilot, following instructions from loved ones.

The situation with Ann Marie's family was difficult. I had met her twin sister a handful of times, but no one else in her family even knew I existed. I had left the decision of whether to introduce me to them up to Ann Marie, as they were her family. And after all, she was a 51-year-old woman who didn't owe her family any explanation other than what she chose to offer. I respected her decisions. Regardless, we needed to get her things ready for them. My sister, rightly so, was not terribly happy with Ann Marie, and begrudged anything I wanted to keep of hers. So I let most everything be packed up, other than a few items, which I kept.

I remember sitting in my office and coming across a small, zippered bag made of suede. It was rectangular and about 6 x 8 inches. The left side was darker greenish brown vertically and the remaining three-quarter portion was a tannish hue with a black star and the word *Vintage* written across the front. As I held the bag, frozen and gazing down at it, the thought went through my mind, *I would like to keep this bag of hers.*

My sister peered over at me and said, "You don't need it. What are you going to do with that?"

I glanced up at her and reluctantly handed the bag over. After packing Ann Marie's items, we drove to my folks' house to get away from the home in which I was reminded of Ann Marie. My family felt that was best, as I still had to hold it together in front of the children, who at the time weren't quite seven years old.

The next day, April 1, while out to eat sushi with my parents and daughters, walking back to our car after dinner, I glanced up and saw a purse just like Ann Marie's hanging in a storefront window. I stopped in my tracks. I took a photo of it and knew Ann Marie was telling me to keep the small purse my sister and I had packed up with her other belongings.

Upon returning to my and Ann Marie's home with my sister, I mentioned the purse and asked if she knew where she had packed it. My sister knew the purse I was talking about and where to find it, even after all the items we had carefully boxed up. She retrieved it for me, and I still have it to this day.

Ann Marie was not a shopper and had this purse for the five years we were together, and who knows how long before I met her. So it is not as if this was a popular purse or an item that was trending at the time. Seeing it in the store window was divine intervention. I was meant to see it. A bonus I later discovered was the little treasure trove of items inside: pens and earbuds. Doesn't sound like a lot, but after returning most of her possessions to her family, they were everything to me.

For me, this happening is not the most miraculous, but it is the first time after Ann Marie's passing that I felt her attempt to communicate with me. I'm not sure why the day before I felt such a strong desire to keep that little purse of hers. Quite a bit of thought had gone into something so minute, compared to all the items we had packed. I felt as if someone were reading my thoughts. Was it Ann Marie? Or maybe God?

April 5, 2019

The First Song

My sister received a phone call from Ann Marie's family, who requested to pick up her items. My sister and I had planned to leave the following morning and meet at the house. We were driving separately, my sister from her home in Sacramento and me from our folks' home in Granite Bay.

I had such trepidation and anxiety on the two-hour drive back home. I asked myself: *Am I going to be able to go back into the house? Am I going to arrive before my sister? If so, should I just wait in my car out front? Should I be brave enough to enter on my own?* Anxiety built inside me with every mile closer to home.

Months prior, my phone had been acting up. One thing you should know about me is that all things tech are foreign to me, especially iPhones. So for me to figure out how to get my Pandora app working again or my iTunes music to play on shuffle was a mystery. Almost home—I remember exactly where I was on Highway 280—my anxiety increasing drastically with every passing minute, my phone went on shuffle and began playing "Just Breathe" (Live Version) by Pearl Jam.

I had not even touched my phone. I had not heard this song in at least 10 years. Honestly, I had never really listened to the words. I had only heard it a handful of times and thought it had a beautiful melody. The lyrics were sung so clearly, I couldn't help but pay attention to them.

After listening to it in awe, a tremendous feeling of peace and strength came over me. I think you will understand why after reading the lyrics.

"Just Breathe" (Live Version) by Pearl Jam

Yes I understand
That every life must end
So as we sit alone,
I know someday we must go
Yeah, I'm a lucky man
To count on both hands
The ones I love
Some folks they have one,
Yeah, others they got none.

Stay with me
Let's just breathe.

Practiced on our sins
Never gonna let me win
Under everything,
Just another human being
Yeah, I don't want to hurt
There's so much in this world
To make me bleed.

Stay with me
You're all I see.

Did I say that I need you?
Did I say that I want you?
Oh, if I didn't, I'm a fool you see
No one knows this more than me
As I come clean.

> I wonder every day
> As I look upon your face
> Everything you gave
> And nothing you would take
>
> Stay with me
> You're all I see.
>
> Did I say that I need you?
> Oh, did I say that I want you?
> Oh, if I didn't, I'm a fool you see
> No one knows this more than me
> As I come clean.
>
> Everything you gave
> Nothing you would take.
> Hold me till I die
> Meet you on the other side.

I cannot begin to describe how every line of this song relates to our relationship and her life. Because of Ann Marie's condition of the mind coupled with self-medicating drinking, our relationship was no walk in the park, but I gave it every fiber of my being. Sometimes, after Ann Marie had an episode, she would come to me on the couch, hold my hand, and tell me she should live alone in a hut on top of a mountain, and that she had behaved like a "fool." She used this word a lot, maybe more than most people.

She had her own distinct way of speaking. When we first met, I thought she sounded like she had just arrived from the 1930s, very proper, but it became so endearing to me. She pronounced every word so clearly. She was bilingual and spoke fluent Spanish. She used old-fashioned terms like "Oh my stars" and "I'm such a fool" and "For Pete's sake" and even "nincompoop." Honestly, when was the last time you heard any of these phrases? I don't think I've heard the word *nincompoop* since I was a child. She also said, "Let us talk." This term always signified to me that she had come back (her mind, that is) from whatever challenging road she had been down, and she was able to speak logically once again.

Often, she was quite empathetic to other people's pain or hardships. If she saw something unkind, she could cry at the drop of a hat. About a week before her passing, she watched the movie *A Star Is Born* with Lady Gaga and Bradley Cooper. I found her crying hysterically and she said, "See! This is why I don't watch movies like this!!"

Ann Marie was a very sensitive soul.

April 11, 2019

The Moth

While picking up our twin girls from kindergarten this day, I was standing outside the classroom door waiting for Nisa and Ella to collect their backpacks and jackets. The teacher, Ms. Ushman, a parent or two, and children were crowded around the doorway trying to say goodbye to each other before heading home.

While I was watching the commotion, I noticed a large white object about the size of a quarter on the carpet. At first, I thought it must be a rubber bug—it was directly between Ms. Ushman's feet, and no one had managed to step on it yet.

When Ella and I made eye contact, I asked what the white thing was on the ground by her feet. One of many things Ann Marie and I had shared was a love of all creatures big and small.

Ella bent over to look and then replied, "A bug!"

I asked her to gently scoop it up before it got stepped on. Everyone was so preoccupied with talking and packing to head home, it was as if Ella and I were having our own private conversation. Miraculously enough, the bug—a moth—had survived all the tromping feet around it. Ella brought the moth over to me and Nisa, and we peered into Ella's hands as she slowly uncupped them.

Now, I don't know about you, but I have never in my life seen a pure, bright-white moth. Not cream-colored or tan. It was all white. It had delicate white fur covering its thorax and abdomen, and the most intricate and unusually large, beautiful antennae. The three of us admired it for a few minutes and gently touched it, as children usually want to touch and feel everything new to them.

It was quite breezy that day, so we released it behind a nearby shed, hoping it would be a safe place.

I knew instantly it was Ann Marie giving me a sign that she was okay. The children were unaware of her passing at this point, so to them it was just a cool bug.

When we arrived home, I googled "moth," and all I could find was an insect named "fluffy moth." It looked very similar to what the children and I had seen. I then searched for the spiritual symbolism behind seeing a white moth, and this is what I found: purity, truth, determination, attraction, psychic ability, faith, and a cleansed Soul.

April 13, 2019

Ann Marie Sighs

At this point, I still had not told my daughters anything about Ann Marie's passing. I was waiting to get into grief counseling for suicide survivors. There, I would be guided on how to tell the children using age-appropriate language and information they could process. As far as they were concerned, Ann Marie had left for Southern California.

The girls were watching the movie *Tooth Fairy* in our bed right below the ceiling fan where Ann Marie had made a failed suicide attempt. (The final act happened outside our bedroom balcony.) While watching the movie, the girls thought they heard Ann Marie sigh twice. It was not a frightening sigh, it was more like a joke, and the children were not afraid in the least.

When I came upstairs to check on them, they told me they had heard Ann Marie. I asked them where the sound came from and how they knew it wasn't just the movie they were watching. They told me it was directly above and a little behind them. It did not come from the TV speakers, and it was Ann Marie's voice.

I believe they truly did hear her.

Ann Marie loved the girls very much, but she was conflicted at times. I think it is possible that the age of our girls at the time of her death may have, unbeknownst to us all, triggered something in her psyche.

Ann Marie was also a twin, which likely stirred up a lot of subconscious and conscious memories of her childhood, along with a host of other circumstances that had transpired. The final straw, I believe, was the fender bender she'd had the day prior to her death, resulting in her being issued a citation for driving under the influence (DUI).

In a letter she wrote to me about a week prior to her passing, she had spoken openly and honestly about her jealousy where the children were concerned. She could not explain why exactly she was experiencing these thoughts and feelings, but she mentioned wanting me to herself. Maybe more telling, she wrote of wondering what it would have been like for her and her sister if they'd had a safe and peaceful home life as children.

She had so many conflicting emotions, but the one thing I know for certain is she loved the girls to her core. She loved—and still loves—all of us.

April 16, 2019

The First Dream

I had my first dream of Ann Marie. She had only been gone at this point for 20 days. But from the moment of her passing, I felt she transitioned immediately.

In my dream, we seemed to be communicating telepathically. I asked if she was going to miss me.

Her reply was, "Yes, but I'm sorry, Jenn, I just had to rip the Band-Aid off …"

When I woke the next morning, I could not help but think, *What an unusual way to describe her actions*. So odd. I gathered that she was in a great deal of mental anguish and had been for most of her life. Life had been a struggle, and she was tired of "practicing on our sins—never gonna let me win."

We had our challenges, our good days, and our bad days. Still, it didn't negate the love and deep connection we felt for each other and the amazing times we had together and as a family.

TUESDAY APRIL 16th, 2019

 I was awakened by a phone call. But I was having a wonderful dream. I asked Ann Marie if she was going to miss me. And she said yes - but she just had to "rip the bandaid off". I asked her for a last kiss and we had one of our slow, sensual kisses. I felt everything. Her beautiful amazing lips. Thank you my love - please visit me again." Roni stayed the night and we had spaghetti for dinner.

WEDNESDAY APRIL 17th, 2019

 Three weeks ago I called 911 at 8:36am. My Love. My darling. This morning I picked up this copy of "Our Daily Bread". It's been sitting on the side table by the couch. I was never interested in it. I don't know why-- I flipped straight to the very back page. And this is what I found. In Ann Marie's hand writing. I could have very easily thrown this into the garbage. Thank you Ann Marie for this.

April 18, 2019

Rip The Band-Aid Off

On April 18, I was getting my hair colored by Katie, my colorist. My philosophy is "Fake it till you make it." So I was doing everything possible to maintain appearances. This had worked for me in the past, and I was doing what I could to regain a sense of normalcy. I had Ann Marie's *Jesus Calling* book with me, her photo, my diary, and a book I was reading about the grieving process by Paula D'Arcy, who lost her husband and young daughter to a drunk driver in 1975. The book was *When People Grieve: Guidance for Grievers and the Friends Who Care*. I've read several of her books and found them to be extremely useful.

Typically, my hair color took quite some time, and Katie and I always had deep conversations about life. While she was working on my hair as usual, we started talking about Ann Marie. Looking back, I am amazed I could act normal and discuss Ann Marie without bursting into tears. I think I must have saved those terrible fits of wailing for my alone times.

Katie said, "Maybe when someone is in that state of mind, they feel people are better off without them, so they just rip the Band-Aid off."

My mouth dropped open. "What made you say that?"

She said, "I don't know. I've never use that saying."

I reached for my diary, went to my second-to-last entry, and pointed to the underlined phrase "rip the Band-Aid off." The exact words Ann Marie had used in my dream to describe why she took her own life.

Katie and I looked at each other with wide eyes, pulled up our sleeves to show each other the chill bumps on our arms, and gazed at each other in mutual shock.

I don't remember the last time I heard someone say that, and I haven't heard it since.

> THURSDAY APRIL 18th, 2019
> Oh my God! Hitting me really hard today. Really really shaky today. Feel sick to my stomach a lot of days. Not feeling good at all. Going to get hair colored. Katie my colorist said maybe when someone is in that state of mind — maybe they feel people are better off without them — so just - (Katie said)
> "rip the bandaid off"
> Rarely do I ever hear this saying but here in the last 2 days - twice. And for Katie to use those words as a discription is so odd. I showed her my journal — she said she never uses that terminology. She didn't know why she said that.

April 25, 2019

The Letter That Wouldn't Stick

In the depths of my grief, I continued to work as best I could. God knows it took everything I had to keep going. Unable to keep work organized, I turned to taping forms from all my approved landscape installation jobs to my office wall. I had between 15 to 20 jobs pending, awaiting the installation phase. This way I could clearly see them at a glance and continue moving forward, even if at a slow pace of completion. At least it was forward and not backward—that is the way I saw it.

This particular day, I stayed home to get office work done. Upon receiving the mail, I opened a letter that looked as if it was from Ann Marie's parents' attorney. It was the second such letter I had received. The first I had ignored and tucked in my drawer about two weeks prior. I was not ready to deal with anything of that nature; it simply broke my heart. I couldn't bear to think about dissolving our assets; they were ours and a part of her.

The letter I received on this day was brief, kindly requesting to have my attorney contact him to discuss the two things Ann Marie and I owned together, our condominium and a beautiful RV we had purchased just two months prior to her death. A barely used 32-foot Chateau with two slides, a full kitchen, two large TVs, and a bathroom. It was gorgeous, and I enjoyed the time I spent stocking it with anything and everything we would possibly need to get away to the coast alone or with the kids.

We'd had big dreams: cooking, reading, walking, and enjoying each other's company. And though I felt the letter had arrived way too soon for my heart's comfort, I knew I could not tuck it away like I had the last. I had to deal with the situation at hand. So I hung it on my wall along with my proposals for upcoming landscape jobs. I moved an existing job on the wall to a different location and put the letter from the attorney in its place.

I answered some emails for a good hour. Needing a refill on my coffee, I went upstairs to the kitchen. When I came back downstairs, I found the letter on the floor. So I carefully taped it back onto the wall for a second time, pressed the tape very firmly with my pointer finger, sat down, and continued with my work.

About an hour later, I needed another coffee refill and headed up the stairs to the kitchen. When I came back down, the letter had fallen once again to the ground. I thought, *I am going to give this letter a run for its money.* In case the paint was preventing it from sticking, even though I'd had a landscape proposal up in the same location for many days prior, I moved it to a different spot. Just to be certain it would not fall again, I added extra strips of tape at the top and bottom of the letter and again pressed firmly to ensure the tape had full and firm contact with the wall.

Some time went by, and I headed upstairs for my third cup of coffee. Upon my return, the letter was, for the third time, on the ground. I said out loud, "Ann Marie, I don't know what you are trying to tell me. Please, I don't understand."

Was I fighting for something she did not want me to have? Or did she want the girls and me to have the condominium? After all, it meant so much to us both, and it was a part of her.

The letter remained in my drawer after that.

The following week, I went out with my crew on my regular Tuesday landscape maintenance route. Many of my customers come out and discuss their gardens with me or simply chat for a bit.

One client, Marcy, was Ann Marie's favorite. I can still hear her voice when we received our Christmas bonus in December of 2018. She said, "I love Marcy. I really do. I mean, she is my favorite." And she had a mutual love affair with Marcy's blind dog, Trixy.

Well, this Tuesday, I told Marcy what had transpired with the letter from the attorney, how it had fallen off my office wall three times. I asked if she thought I might be losing it, or did she also see it as some form of communication or sign, and if so, what could Ann Marie be trying to tell me?

Marcy also believed it was a sign but could not understand what Ann Marie was attempting to make me notice.

Marcy was aware of the battle I faced, trying to somehow hold on to the condominium. After all, I would never be able to get back into the housing market again in the Bay Area. Homes are simply too expensive here. Keeping it would provide financial security and peace of mind for the girls and me. A place to live that would be stable and manageable as far as the mortgage payment, as we had a 30-year fixed rate. It was in a top-notch school district, and I felt very safe there—alone, and with the kids. On top of that, it would be a wonderful long-term investment and provide security in my retirement years. Being able to hold on to the condominium would change our lives drastically.

A week went by, and Tuesday rolled around again. Marcy came out to chat. "You know, Jenn, I've been thinking about what you told me last week, and what Ann Marie is trying to communicate to you." Then she asked, "How are you listed on the deed?"

I told Marcy I had no idea. I mean, who knows that? She told me that she used to do probate work, and if we were listed as "joint tenancy," the condominium would be mine solely, where tenancy in common would mean, I would have to sell. If joint tenancy, I would not have to sell it and split the proceeds with Ann Marie's parents or consider my other option of trying to buy them out. The second option was unlikely, as I did not have enough cash in the bank.

I immediately called my real estate agent, who is also a friend, and asked if there would be any way for him to find out how Ann Marie and I were listed on the deed. I explained that it could potentially be amazing news for me if we were listed as joint tenancy. He said he would get right on it. I did not have high hopes, but I thought it sure would remove a lot of stress in my life and was worth checking out.

My attorney would not know anything about joint tenancy, as he is my brother-in-law, who was helping me out of the kindness of his heart. He had a full plate running his firm and was in an entirely different area of law.

By day's end, I had heard back from Jeremy, my real estate agent.

"Jenn, great news! You are listed as joint tenancy."

"The good one! So I don't have to sell?"

"No, you don't have to sell!"

If it weren't for that letter falling off my wall three times and Marcy's help, I would never have been able to hold on to our condominium. The chain of events that unraveled here was uncanny. If that letter had not fallen from the wall so many times, if I had not told Marcy what had happened, if Marcy had not known about joint tenancy, I would not have received such a life-altering gift.

I truly, honestly, and wholeheartedly believe Ann Marie wanted us to have the condominium, to provide a secure future for the girls and me. Equally important, I have a piece of my and Ann Marie's life together. Some of my best memories were made there with Ann Marie and the girls. She wanted to take care of her family. And she has done that.

May 16, 2019

OUR HOME Pin On A Map

I felt a lot of anxiety on this day. Ann Marie's birthday was only four days away. (She was a Taurus.)

Again, I am not very good with my iPhone or computer; I just know some basics. One app I use is Maps, as I do a lot of driving and frequently meet with potential customers. But on this particular evening, I attended my first suicide survivor support group meeting. After the meeting, I got in my car and entered my address into the app so I could drive home.

Out of nowhere, a small pin with a red head appeared onscreen. It had Ann Marie's photo and her name—its location labeled as OUR HOME.

I had never pinned anything before. Didn't even know how. I was so shocked to see her name and photo that I stared at my phone for a moment trying to figure out how it had appeared. I did not think to snap a screenshot of it. Ann Marie was letting me know she was with me—everywhere. She was at home, where I felt her the most in those early days, months, and years.

May 20, 2019

A Ladybug With Heart

I am compelled to write about Ann Marie's birthday. To me, the events of that day were heaven-sent. In the days leading up to her birthday, I was feeling anxious. You see, I had been shunned by her old friends from Southern California, who didn't even know me. I had no communication with her family. There was a horrific rumor circulating in certain crowds that I had been involved in her death, the details of which I will not mention. I received unthinkably cruel text messages from these "friends." I was not included in any type of Life Celebration ceremonies.

To try and cope with Ann Marie's death and then all this cruelty was unbearable. There were a few people, at most, I could share my overwhelming feelings of grief with. I could only imagine that for some reason God wanted me to experience this heartbreak, for the most part, on my own. I did not understand why. So I relied on trust and faith in God and the universe that someday I would understand.

The evening before Ann Marie's birthday, it came to me: I had let God, Jesus, and the universe guide me thus far, so I should just let the day take its course and see what was sent to me from above. Let everything go and simply flow.

I began Ann Marie's birthday with some journaling, a time I treasured. I set aside every spare moment. If a day or two went by without journaling, I felt overwhelming anxiety.

I started my journaling on this day with something Ann Marie often said to me, "Don't drown in a glass of water, Jenn."

I wrote a bit more, then set it aside for more journaling later in the day. I decided to go on one of our favorite hikes. We used to hike just about every weekend or whenever we had spare time. A beautiful hike with amazing views, gorgeous oak trees, green grasses, and a plethora of wildflowers in the spring. I had left my reading glasses in my car but took my phone with me on the hike. My intention was to reach the 200-foot white cross that stands atop a mountain, which you can see across the expansive canyon from our home.

While on my hike, I noticed a big, red ladybug directly in my path. I snapped a photo and continued my hike. A short while later, I made it to the cross, or awfully close. I took a few photos of the cross and turned to head back down the mountain trail, all the while wondering if Ann Marie's footsteps had ever landed where mine were. That's something I think about a lot. *That rock or tree is still here, and Ann Marie isn't. How can that be?*

As I walked back, the clouds looked so heavenly rolling over the mountains that separated us by just a few miles as the crow flies from the Pacific Coast. Since I did not have my reading glasses, I was blindly snapping photos of whatever looked interesting or beautiful to me, but with no real visual clarity while looking at my phone.

Having made it back to my car, I headed home. I retrieved the mail and started thumbing through it when I noticed a return address that I did not recognize. The envelope contained a handwritten note along with a small photo of Ann Marie with her name, birth, and death years written on it. There was also a beautiful picture of Jesus, which had printed on it "Jesus, I Trust in You." A third photo featured a white dove in flight with a background of such a pale blue as to be almost white and written on the back was a short prayer for Ann Marie.

The note read: "I am returning this note to you. Was found by me in the rented car in Millbrae. Sorry for your loss. With warm regards, Ms. Maria."

I can only imagine that Ann Marie's mother had dropped it in the car she had rented when she was here to take care of the funeral arrangements. Receiving this note in the mail on Ann Marie's birthday meant everything to me, and was only the first sign that God, Jesus, and Ann Marie were with me on this day of her birth. I was not remembering and celebrating her alone.

Later, I decided to do a little office work, even if only to stay caught up with emails. Sitting at my desk, I reached into the small drawer to the right of my computer. I honestly do not know what I was looking for or even why I would go to the back corner of my desk drawer with my hand. After all, I knew everything that was in there. It has always been my stapler, a three-hole punch, stamps, return address stickers, and a bottle of Wite-Out Ann Marie had purchased.

But what I pulled out was an amazing treasure. A small 2½ x 3-inch lime-green-and-blue tin box with "Nut Case" printed on the front.

I had never seen it before. I opened it and found several wallet-size photos of Mother Teresa with a prayer written on the back; a half-dozen small medallions with "PRAY FOR US" printed on one side; two of Ann Marie's business cards (a side career she'd had selling health insurance in addition to her day job as a family nurse practitioner); and last, but not least, her rosary.

Finding this small box of hers was the greatest gift I could have hoped for. It held meaningful items and had found its way to me on such an auspicious day. Even though I had been shunned by most, the only one who mattered to me was making it abundantly clear she was watching over me and comforting me at this significant moment in time.

After what I had felt was a perfect day celebrating Ann Marie, I sat on the couch to start a movie, but before doing so I thought I would take a gander at the photos I had snapped on my hike. I put my reading

 glasses on and opened my phone. I was taken aback by the ladybug I had photographed; it had an unmistakable big, black heart on its back. Scrolling through the few photos I had taken of the clouds, one stood out immediately. I saw three angels and two hearts. Upon closer inspection, I found more hearts and a very clear cloud that formed two of Ann Marie's Chihuahua pups, which had passed while we were together.

My friend Liam called as I was making this discovery, so I texted her the photo. I was so amazed at what I was seeing, I was compelled to share this incredible photo. My friend had known it was Ann Marie's birthday and that it might be a tough day for me, so she reached out. She studies clouds a lot and said it was the most amazing one she had seen to date, with so much symbolism. She sent me a marked-up text of the photo with all the angels and hearts outlined.

 I shed a lot of tears that day. Tears of gratitude. Tears of missing Ann Marie's physical presence. I thanked Jesus and Ann Marie for all the miracles they had sent me. I felt showered with love from the Other Side. My heart overflowed with love and gratitude. Even though Ann Marie was not physically with me, she was with me still.

May 27, 2019

Death By A Thousand Cuts

One thing that was especially hard for me was losing establishments that Ann Marie and I had frequented. I felt like my memories with her were slowly being chipped away. When I saw our local Subway sandwich shop closed, I was heartbroken. One more place of "ours" was gone. Like her.

On this particular Monday, I drove down to our massage salon. I hadn't been there since Ann Marie passed. I knew it was going to be a big step for me walking through those doors. My mind's eye kept seeing her sitting on the couch waiting for our appointment. Seeing her beautiful arm draped down from beneath the sheet of her massage table. I was now doing our weekly routine alone.

As I walked up to the large glass door and pulled on the door handle, it did not budge. I looked around in confusion, and then saw a sign in the window that read "Out of Business." I called the number on the door several times but only got a voicemail. I left several messages with no response.

I was devastated. Like the Taylor Swift song "Death By A Thousand Cuts." We used to get foot and back massages every week, alternating Saturday and Sunday, directly after dropping our girls off at my ex's. The East West Foot Spa held such great significance for me. After our massages every week, we would go home and crawl into bed, order

Chinese food, turn on a movie, and fall asleep. Ann Marie was quite ritualistic. Neither of us minded a consistent schedule; in fact, we both thrived with one. For some it might seem boring, but not for us.

After finding that our spa had closed, I drove home and poured my sadness into my journal. I always ended my journaling by giving thanks to God and Jesus, and with "I love you, Ann Marie" and a heart next to her name.

I prayed that I could somehow get in contact with the owner so I could tell her of Ann Marie's passing.

The next day, I stopped to get cash at a Chase Bank, five cities away from where Ann Marie and I resided and our spa was located. I had never been there before. While at the ATM, deep in thought as I often was that first year, I heard someone yell, "Jennifer!" I looked around to see who was calling my name, and there she was walking toward me, the owner of the spa. I am sorry to say I do not remember her name. (Unlike me, Ann Marie always knew everyone's name and always used it—it was very personable. I loved that about her.)

I hugged the woman and told her of Ann Marie's passing. She was very sad and shocked to hear the news. We talked for a while. She asked if Ann Marie was in her forties, but I told her Ann Marie had been 54 at the time of her death. (I had to include that in the day's diary entry because that comment would have thrilled Ann Marie.) I had a photo of Ann Marie with me as I always did, and I gave it to the owner of our spa.

Once again, the universe answered my simple prayer. Simple yet so important to the process of my healing and my uncharted grief. Ann Marie was granting my every wish.

June 17, 2019

First Reading With Kay Fahlstrom, In Person
Sonoma, California

As I mentioned, I tackled my grief from every angle possible. This included readings from three different psychic mediums. All my readings were amazingly, unmistakably accurate, and packed with so much information.

My first reading was in person with a woman named Kay. Ann Marie had a lot she wanted to communicate to me, and with Kay's help, she was able to do so. The following is transcribed from my first reading with Kay.

KAY: We are mostly doing all mediumship today. I'm hearing from somebody who crossed over. Although there is more than one, I feel like. It is not an exact science because they decide who comes through and in which order, not the medium. So even if you have the world's best medium, the people in Spirit decide who comes through. But I can still try to tune in on who you want.

How it works is we are in a three-dimensional world [*she knocked on a wood chair*] because we have heavy trucks, cars, and furniture all having density, width, weight, and mass. They are beyond the three-dimensional world. So it's kinda trippy to think about, but they do not have this form and density and heaviness. So they are at a much higher, faster vibration. Think about a hummingbird's wings going super fast.

Or science class: solids, liquids, gases. You keep going up in speed and vibration and BOOP—you are past 3-D and on the Other Side, which is four dimensions or more. So they have to come way down, and I have to go way up, for us to hear bits and snippets.

I don't hear complete paragraphs, no medium does. We get images and pictures, we hear stuff, we feel things with our body, and we feel the emotion of how they feel and all that. So that's called clairvoyance, clairaudience, clairsentience. It's our regular senses but extrasensory. It's like we can hear in our head from the Other Side.

So having said all that, let's get started. I feel a couple people in Spirit. You want to hear mainly from one person, right?

ME: Yes.

KAY: I say, "Come on, show me who you are." I ask them to stand in a specific spot. It's kind of like if you put a family tree around my body. Your dad would be up on the left. Your mom would be up to the right. This is the parent level. To your side would be like a brother, sister, or spouse. Then below would be a child.

The person is on your level, not a parent, not a child who passed; I feel [this person] is extremely close to you. Cares about you so much. I feel it was someone who passed younger than most. Is that right?

ME: Yeah.

KAY: Okay. Hang on a second. I'm going to ask some questions of them. [*A few moments of silence*] I feel like she's a close friend. Not a sister. Is that right?

ME: Right.

KAY: Okay. Were you guys involved romantically?

ME: Yeah.

KAY: Okay, very good. So I feel like we are so close, like a spouse. Okay. We've got someone close, like a spouse. I feel like someone you were dating, or your spouse, has passed. She's showing as somebody who passes younger than most. I hear from them loud and clear. This is good. There's this feeling right off the bat, this is her. "You're so beautiful. You look so beautiful." Like right off the bat. She's so happy that you are here today. She says, "It isn't all wasted." Okay. "My passing. It is not all wasted. Our relationship, it's not all wasted." She says, "There's a purpose for all this. I'll explain." She goes more into explaining. "It has been revealed to me that there is a purpose for the age that I passed at." She's bringing this up and she goes more into it later.

As you know, I channeled before you arrived, and I have my notes, but I receive more messages for you while we are together. I feel like the passing was pretty recent. I feel like less than six months. Is it like two or three weeks or months?

ME: Three months.

KAY: Wow. Very recent. I'm so sorry. I'm so very sorry. She's saying the misery will lift over time. She knows how upset you've been. Okay. "I don't want you to feel that forever." Now, easy for them to say because you're the one grieving. She wants to say some things about her physical body. I feel like she's talking about some kind of issue in the head to neck area. I also feel like there's this feeling of possibly drugs or alcohol. Some kind of substance that altered her thoughts. 'Cause there's a feeling of … "I would think about things in a negative way. And I don't know if you knew that or not?"

ME: Yes.

KAY: You did. Okay, because sometimes we don't know someone's innermost thoughts. But I'm hearing from her "There was a way in which I saw some things negatively or I would perseverate—it went around and around and around." Do you understand? And so then she's saying, "It kind of added to what was going on and then it made me feel worse." I talk about the head and neck area. That might just be the altered thoughts. I don't know if it was drugs or alcohol, but something was influencing the way she thought negatively. Okay. She's saying ... she says she had nagging doubts that plagued her.

ME: About our relationship?

KAY: NO!! About the way that she thought ... about herself. About her and the world. About earlier experiences in her life. It kind of set up this thought loop. She's saying—I don't know if this is a metaphor or literal—"I walked out into a faulty space." Or "I kind of got myself out into a precarious area." You know. It could just be a metaphor for "I got myself out into a precarious area." She's saying something like "I was a hair's breadth away from this not happening. I was so close to this not happening, but then it happened."

So it's very interesting to me, because I can usually feel the difference between somebody who passes from a disease, someone who passed from an accident, and someone who is responsible for their own passing. You understand? They are usually in one category or another. I feel like this is blended. And there's just kind of a mixture. I feel like she was not responsible for her own passing, but when I keep asking, "Is this a disease or an accident?" it just doesn't feel super clear to me. She also gives me this feeling of like split open.

ME: She … um … she … um. Okay.

KAY: What happened? She is saying, "I'm sorry," which is usually something a Spirit says when they are responsible for their own passing. She's just talking about how her thoughts got so bad.

ME: Yeah.

KAY: And "I got myself out into a precarious space." Does this make sense? What … what happened to her?

ME: She … she … um … attempted to hang herself from the ceiling fan.

KAY: That's the head and the neck because she's making me feel like that.

ME: Then she … it didn't work.

KAY: She says, "I was a hair's breadth away from not doing it, then I did it. I'm sorry."

ME: Then she went out onto the balcony, and she hung herself.

KAY: Oh my God, Jenn.

ME: In our bedroom.

KAY: So that's why I keep flashing to my new best friend in Sacramento; she did the same thing. So they kept making me see my good friend Sue, who did the same thing.

So these are very unique things to hear. When I hear "I'm sorry," that takes me to "I'm responsible for my own passing." Spirits don't like to say the word "suicide." I don't care who has crossed over. They don't like to say the S word. And I don't know if that's because they are so loved on the Other Side with compassion that the people on the Other Side say you don't have to call it that. But then I'm like, was this a disease or an accident or a suicide? I feel like she was kind of all over the place. Did she have drugs or alcohol adding to things?

ME: Yes.

KAY: Okay. So that's a point of proof. So that altered her thoughts and made it worse, sadly. She is just so sorry. She feels so bad about all of this. She's saying, "I am sorry I left you with such an experience." She wants to say, "I ingested the [whatever] regularly. That altered my thoughts." So she's basically talking about something that regularly altered her thoughts. And she's saying, "I perseverated. I kept going around and around with the thoughts."

ME: Is she at peace?

KAY: She's saying yes and no. She's saying, "Yes, I'm at peace, but I am still working on [*this is a weird word*] unpacking the trauma." So she is working on healing. Also, she's been there such a short time. A lot of the two- to three-month time frame, even more, can be looking at how that affected you. Like she might just be looking at that for quite a while. She's coming to terms with the impact it made on you and other people, and that's a perfectly normal thing to be doing in the first two to three months.

She says, "This is going to change both of us, not for the bad but for the better." Again, she knows the pain, she's not making light of what happened, but there's this thing about this huge growth that's going to happen as a result.

She says, "I can see you're already considering new things … you're open to new ideas." She keeps talking about that. The growth that's going to happen because of it. That's why she said it's not all wasted. There's a point to all this, which is growth. She's showing tremendous growth, because I feel like you are open to more ideas now about what is real—the Other Side. You already see that.

She's still sorry she did it and devastated you. She said, "I blew things out of proportion. I saw the negative of things at times." I said, "Give me your personality. Tell me, were you gregarious, loud, this or that?" She's talking about her innermost thoughts a lot. And how that was a huge burden. You could see where it went back to. She said, "It was no way to be."

I asked her how she comes through to you. And she said, "Yesterday. I was trying to come through to you yesterday." Out in nature, it's easier for her to come through to you. Though it doesn't mean she can't come through to you in the house. She can do that also. She's showing birds, butterflies, hummingbirds, dragonflies, and I especially feel butterflies and dragonflies. She also makes you hear … this is how she comes through to you and tries to get your attention and say, "Hi, I'm here. I love you. We are still connected." She makes you hear music and certain songs and certain genres. So it's the band—not just this band, not just this song—but it's Fleetwood Mac.

ME: Oh, really. That's my favorite band!

KAY: And like some rock and roll, and some newer stuff too.

ME: Uh-huh.

KAY: It's the whole lexicon of music. She can use any modern song or goes all the way back to like good oldies. She made me hear a Stevie Nicks song.

ME: Oh, there's a song by Fleetwood Mac … "I go into her closet, and I smell her hat every day, but the smell is starting to fade." And there is a lyric somewhere. It's a Stevie Nicks song that just plays in my head: "Your softness fades away." [*I'm sobbing, almost unable to get the words out.*]

KAY: She must have said Fleetwood Mac because she knows you like that band. And she made me hear a Stevie Nicks song. So she knows about that song, and she knows that you are hearing that in your head when you smell her hat. She also comes through with electronics. She messes with electronics. I feel like you are going to have some stuff happen on your phone or computer or things like that, that aren't even possible on the phone or computer. And she picks different songs for you to hear. She's trying to get you certain songs to say, "Hi, I'm here. I still love you."

She's also showing me ladybugs, grasshoppers, crickets. The people in Spirit can influence the animal to come into your field of vision. She's influencing the butterflies, the birds, and all these little guys. She's saying, "I was." Some people are just left-brain or right-brain. They are super analytical—accountants or poetic, creative people, and stuff like that. She says, "I was both." She had both. She had elements of both. She could be analytical and yet she could be creative too. She could think in both ways.

She says I was … I was … [*Kay laughs.*] This is so cool. I thought we were done with the "tell me something specific" part of the reading, but she keeps talking. She says, "I WAS TERRITORIAL. SHE WAS MINE!"

ME: Yes! Ann Marie was territorial.

KAY: Like nobody was flirting with you! [*more laughter*]

ME: No. Huh-uh.

KAY: She says, "I was territorial. She was mine." I'm like, "GOT IT!" She did NOT want anyone else flirting with you or even trying. Ann Marie is saying, "The mechanism of our connection—of our love—was the heart. There was no explanation needed." She's saying, "Nature." When you're quiet, it's easier for her to get through to you. So phones, radios, TVs—turn all that junk off if you want to hear from Ann Marie more easily. It's so much easier for her to get through to you. When we are just spacing out even. Boop! They can go thought to thought with us. "When you're crying on the bed and looking up, I'm there with you."

So she is visiting all over the place. In nature. When you're watering or irrigating, or I don't know what you do with your business, but she's with you when you are doing your job. And visiting. You two have a very good connection. She's saying, "My personality over here is making sense of how short my life was. I was just getting started." But then there's another part where the Soul of Ann Marie is like, "Oh, I kind of signed up for a shorter life." And then there's the purpose of it. Like then it's going to cause this huge growth in you, then your daughters are going to grow up knowing that this kind of stuff can happen. The kids are actually more amazing because they've had an early loss. And so, there's a purpose to all of it. Your Soul. Your kids' Souls.

She's joking about herself. Ann Marie is hilarious [*laughing*]. She is saying, "I was a bit like a caveman." Simple needs [*more laughing from Kay*]. Like "I'm attracted to you. I want really good food." You know [*laughing*]. "I'm thirsty." Like, there's this part of Ann Marie that is

"I'm simple. This is what I want." But she was also this well-developed, creative person. She was all these wonderful things. She's just totally cracking a joke [*Kay laughing*]. So she's just hilarious. She's so fun because she's joking around. You can hear she is literally telling me what to say, and she's just talking as fast as she can. She says, "Jenn, I love you." She says, "Don't drown in your sorrows. I'm still here and we are still connected. Our love doesn't change. We can communicate at any time."

ME: Okay.

KAY: Do you have a picture of Ann Marie? Can I see a picture of her? Would you allow me to do that?

ME: I do. [*I hand photos to Kay.*]

KAY: IS THIS HER?!

ME: Yeah.

KAY: Oh my God. WOW. You guys are awesome. What a big, beautiful love. Thank you so much for sharing these with me. I can't describe how it is to hear somebody. And you can also get bits and pieces of her personality. And then to see a picture is just so gratifying.

ME: [*I hand Kay another photo of Ann Marie.*] This is one of my favorite pictures. She was happy here. She was helping my dad at the vineyard.

KAY: I have to say, you guys kind of look like … Do you mind me saying this? You two look like Sandra Bullock and Julia Roberts.

ME: [*I chuckle shyly.*]

KAY: Do people say that?

ME: People thought she was Sandra Bullock or Julia Roberts. She got that all the time. Especially at LAX [Los Angeles International Airport]. A few times reporters ran up to her thinking she was a movie star only to be disappointed. We always laughed about that.

KAY: Right. But you look like Julia Roberts.

ME: I never get that.

KAY: Ann Marie is funny. I feel like she was feminine but also capable and could do things—like you can. You both are like that. But she's also saying, "I'm getting my sensitivity; it's developing more over here." There is the emotional sensitivity, spiritual growth, and learning. And she's saying over and over "And that's the point of the early separation." As devastating as it is.

And she is with a new community on the Other Side. She's not going away from you. But I feel now she has the support of grandparents. And then she's continuing to love you and will continue to guide and love the girls. She says, "We are always connected. Our love will never change." It's like a chain link that you can't ever change. It's a massive love.

June 24, 2019

Grief Deepens You

I tackled my grieving and loss head on. Honestly, I didn't know what else to do. I made certain to get a weekly massage. Ann Marie and I had an extremely active love life, and I didn't think it healthy to go cold turkey and not have any human touch. The massages also calmed and relaxed my nerves. I am certain I had post-traumatic stress disorder (PTSD). Loud noises would startle my entire body, and I had never been one to scare easily prior to Ann Marie's passing.

The week after Ann Marie's death, I started back up with a psychotherapist, the same person who had helped me through my divorce. I needed to talk. It was and still is a wonderful space to get it all out. I did group counseling with other suicide survivors. In fact, I participated in two different group counseling arenas where I could hear other perspectives, thoughts, and feelings of others who had lost a loved one to suicide. Not many, though, saw this as a spiritual awakening. In all my meetings, I met three other women who'd had spiritual experiences and saw the divine in what had happened. But I only did the group therapy for a few months. I just didn't feel it was the space for me, although I am very grateful to the amazing people who facilitated the groups.

One woman I would like to thank is Isabel. At the start of one of our sessions, she read aloud a passage that meant so much to me, from *The Power Deck* by Lynn V. Andrews. I've included it here:

> Grief deepens you. It allows you to explore the perimeters of your soul. Grief is the only gateway to certain levels of consciousness, and it is a hard taskmaster. Through grief you can explore every aspect of your dark side—anger, pain, abandonment, terror, loneliness—and these are aspects of the sacred wound that in our daily lives we usually try to ignore. Grief forces you to look at those parts of yourself that are not yet healed. If you can look at grief as a teaching, you will grow. The pain of grief is not the only teacher in this life, but if looked at properly, with awareness and an open heart, it is one of the greatest teachers of all. The seeds of wisdom and enlightenment are planted within the wounds of grief. What is lost can only come back to us again in higher ways.

This passage spoke to me. It was exactly what I was experiencing, and I was so grateful to hear it. At times, I thought there was something wrong with me. I felt isolated from other suicide survivors. I didn't understand how they were unable to see a great miracle through tragedy. A gift. Someone had died. Please use this opening to connect with God and your loved one.

Don't misunderstand me. I was heartbroken, quite literally my heart and chest hurt every day, but I also felt this amazingly overwhelming sense of peace, love, and connection to everything in the universe. It's the only way I can describe it. Ann Marie sacrificed her life. She granted me this gift. I could not dishonor her by not accepting it.

I also did a more physical form of PTSD therapy called synergy reset with Angelica. I sought out mediums and psychics. I found three I really liked and to date have had amazing readings. I tried very hard to get proper sleep and forced myself to eat. But I still lost 30 pounds. I read a lot of books. I couldn't read them fast enough. Typically, I am not a big reader; I never have been. I am dyslexic. But I must have read at least 5 books on grieving and 30 or so that were either channeled or about life after death.

On this date, June 25, 2019, I had my first reading with a psychic named Sandra O'Hara. I taped all my readings so I could listen to them again, as the sessions can be quite overwhelming. It can be a lot of information coming at you quickly. In this reading, Sandra had said, "Ann Marie is showing me a squirrel. I have no idea why, but she is showing me a squirrel. I have never been shown a squirrel before. Do you make anything of that?"

Just the day prior, June 24, I had traveled hundreds of miles to meet with Angelica, who would be guiding me through PTSD therapy. She is a very kind and gentle woman with loads of wisdom and knowledge, eager to share with anyone who needs advice, and is willing to listen. She is grounded and aware and found a way through her own traumatic childhood to grow and expand her consciousness. After a long drive and arriving four hours early, we finally met at a mutual acquaintance's home. We decided to sit outside on the backyard patio to get to know each other before starting my session.

As we talked, I shared about my loss and the circumstances surrounding it. About 30 minutes in, we were distracted to the point of complete silence, for what seemed like quite some time, by a squirrel. I don't think either of us had ever seen anything quite like it. It was a rather large, gray squirrel with a sweeping, fluffy, beautiful tail. It is difficult to describe its behavior, but this squirrel was hanging onto a four-foot chain-link fence, as if she were begging us to notice her. She was darting up and forward, then down and forward rapidly, and repeating this for a very long time, in what seemed like no specific direction.

After a few minutes of watching, I began to speak again. I felt a little uncomfortable with the attention we were giving this extremely entertaining squirrel, but Angelica could not pull her attention or eyes away from the comical dance the squirrel was putting on for us. Eventually, she refocused on our conversation.

I'll never forget it. I told Sandy about that squirrel encounter. She said, "That was Ann Marie."

People who have passed are able to influence insects and animals to enter a person's field of vision. Sandra was spot-on about that and everything else in my reading.

June 25, 2019

First Reading With Sandra O'Hara, Via Skype

SANDRA: Are you a twin? Or are there twins somewhere? They are showing me twins.

ME: I have twin daughters. Six and a half years old.

SANDRA: Okay. They may be twins, but they are very, very different from each other is what I am told. Totally different personalities, and I feel that one of them has this wisdom where she'll come out with something like "Oh my God—how did she know that? And the other one is very bright also—very intelligent but she likes to kind of sit back and observe things before she makes a move.

Your grandmother is showing me a broken relationship. But she's telling me that you are NAVIGATING this quite well. Have you stepped out into the dating game again?

ME: Well … I was hoping to kind of reach out to someone I lost recently, and … ah.

SANDRA: Right. Okay.

ME: It's only been three months and … I'm ah, you know, grieving.

SANDRA: Yeah. I understand. And who had the tragic passing, please? The death was upsetting. There's like a tragedy connected to this, and it's giving me a feeling of [this person] being responsible for it. Does that make sense?

ME: [*I nod.*]

SANDRA: Mmkay. And I feel it's her energy that's coming in and she's saying, "Happy birthday." So whose birthday has just passed or just coming up?

ME: My sister's.

SANDRA: Your sister—okay. And she's also giving me feelings that she passed around the time it's normally celebrated. So I don't know if she means by the public or she means by family. So when your partner passed, was it around something that should have been celebrated?

ME: Around her birthday.

SANDRA: Around her birthday. Okay. And she's also telling me to tell you that she heard your goodbyes, that guilt is unnecessary. So you seem to be carrying guilt, and she's telling me that is unnecessary.

And she's talking about the sharp words. So had you had some sharp words just before she passed?

ME: [*I nod again.*]

SANDRA: Yeah. So your head is probably replaying that, and it's like she is saying, "Please don't do that." Do you know what I mean? It was not the reason that what happened, happened.

And she's also showing me what looks like letters. So do you have letters from her? Or cards? Or something that she wrote?

ME: Yes. I journal every day, and I've got all of her Post-its, and I stick them inside my journal.

SANDRA: Yeah. Because I feel that she's around you when you do that. Mmkay.

And she is showing me a lot to do with music as well, so there was a love for music, or she was into music. She sends signs to you through music. So you might hear something that is from her or about her music-wise. It's like, "Yes that's me—I'm here."

There is something about the way she was found. I don't know quite what she is trying to tell me. She's only passed three months, is that what you said? So three months to us is like three hours to her. Do you know what I mean? And this is all very fresh for her, so there's just something about the way she was found … and she's very sorry for that. Does that make sense?

ME: [*I nod.*]

SANDRA: Had there been a little bit of an age difference?

ME: She won't like me saying this, but she was five years older.

SANDRA: Right. Okay. Well, she's laughing about it. She's laughing about it and she just says, "Let's not split hairs." And [*laughing hard*] … she's also mentioning the name Mary to me. Who's Mary?

ME: [*long pause*] Maybe her mom or grandmother?

SANDRA: Right. Was there some division with them?

ME: [*pause*] Ah … yes, she had suffered abuse.

SANDRA: At the hands of her mother?

ME: Yeah. [*softly and somewhat ashamed*] I never met her parents.

SANDRA: Yup. I just feel as if this is something that kind of dogged her all her life, if I can say that. So even before you met her, there were these mental health issues going on that were connected to dark times in her life. And she says you did bring light into her life. And that she's sorry she didn't stay longer. Again, she wants you not to take blame or be guilty about her passing.

Then she's showing me a China cup. Why is she showing me a China cup?

ME: [*pause with disbelief*] A China cup. I … we painted one of the bedrooms together, and I just moved the China cup we had used for that today. I was going to throw it away, but I held on to it because … she had held it.

SANDRA: The China cup?

ME: Yeah. It has dried purple paint in it.

SANDRA: Yeah. So I think she was around today when you were thinking about doing that. Now she doesn't mind whether you throw it away or you don't, but if it has sentimental value for you, please hold on to it. But it doesn't matter if you do throw it out because the memory is there nonetheless.

Okay. She is a very attractive lady. But she tells me she had a very checkered background.

ME: [*I hold up a photo of Ann Marie.*] Can you see that?

SANDRA: Oh WOW!! She's a beautiful lady. Absolutely stunning. But she's telling me she had a checkered background. So she didn't tell everybody her story, as it were.

She is also telling me about not just the abusive relationship within her family in her young years but also, she was in an abusive romantic relationship as well. So does that make sense?

ME: Mmm. [*I nod.*]

SANDRA: Okay. So all of these kinds of things led her to the path that she took. She keeps showing me a lot of medication. Had she been taking a lot of medication?

ME: Yeah.

SANDRA: She's giving me a feeling of chronic pain. Does that make sense?

ME: She had been working with me for the last, uh … nine months, and her knee was really bothering her. I do landscaping and gardening, and we thought pulling her out of the office would give her some peace, being outdoors.

SANDRA: Yeah. Mmm.

ME: Her knee really started bothering her.

SANDRA: Yeah. She's also showing me cherry blossoms. Does that mean anything to you?

ME: Our sushi restaurant has a huge glass mural of two cherry trees in bloom flanking a snowcapped mountain. It takes up three walls.

SANDRA: Okay. But she told me she was in chronic pain and that she used to self-medicate with the chronic pain, you know, and she said that was not helpful either. But she's also giving me a strong smell of alcohol, so she would have drunk more than she needed to drink.

She is very thankful for the time that you had together and allowing her into your daughters' lives, and she's blowing you a kiss. And the other thing I would say to you is, she's also showing me a squirrel? I have no idea why she is showing me a squirrel! It might make sense, or it might be a memory. I have no idea.

ME: I … yesterday … I went to the city of Novato for … I think it's called TLR trauma therapy, and Angelica (my therapist) and I watched a squirrel for quite a while on a fence. It was really funny. It was on a chain-link fence, and it was crawling really fast and erratic.

SANDRA: I think that was your partner.

ME: The squirrel?

SANDRA: Yes.

ME: Making Angelica and me laugh?

SANDRA: Yup.

ME: We watched it for quite a while.

SANDRA: I think it was her. Absolutely.

July 2, 2019

My Heart Still Hurts

On this day, my journal begins like this: "My heart still hurts—most days it feels like a knife has been plunged into my chest. I still can't believe you are gone, my darling. How will I go on without you? I loved you—love you so. I just keep going. Doing my best every day."

The day before this entry, I had a longtime friend and colleague in my office. We were doing something on my computer when it just froze. The cursor was nowhere to be found on the screen, and this song began playing.

"Everything I Own" by Bread

You sheltered me from harm
Kept me warm, kept me warm
You gave my life to me
Set me free, set me free
The finest years I ever knew
Were all the years I had with you

And I would give anything I own
I'd give up my life, my heart, my home
I would give everything I own
Just to have you back again

You taught me how to love
What it's of, what it's of

> You never said too much
> But still you showed the way
> And I knew from watching you
> Nobody else could ever know
> The part of me that can't let go
>
> And I would give anything I own
> I'd give up my life, my heart, my home
> I would give everything I own
> Just to have you back again
>
> Is there someone you know
> You're loving them so
> But taking them all for granted?
> You may lose them one day
> Someone takes them away
> And they don't hear the words you long to say
>
> I would give anything I own
> I'd give up my life, my heart, my home
> I would give everything I own
> Just to have you back again
> Just to touch you once again

I remember vividly a day when Ann Marie was angry with me for something. I decided to ignore her, take a bubble bath, and listen to my music. I was playing some oldies, one of which was that song by Bread.

She came into the bathroom, held my hand, and said, "I'm so sorry, Jenn. I love you so. I know how blessed I really am."

When Ann Marie was alive, I used to put my Bose headset over her ears and play songs for her that were special to me. I never said too much, but I did try to gently help her feelings of discontentment.

One day, I asked her to lie on the bed in the spare bedroom where it was quiet. I put my headset on her head and played one of my favorite songs for her, "Ordinary Miracle" by Sarah McLachlan. She loved it. I feel blessed that I was able to share that with her.

For two people who only had five years together, we really covered a lot of territory. I even told her that if the world were to end and we were not together, my last thoughts and love would be with her.

July 7, 2019

Breathing You In

The following is my journal entry from July 7, 2019:

"I started putting your pictures in an album today, my love. Of course, I had my iTunes playing on shuffle. I only recently have been able to listen to other genres of music. For many months, all I could handle was my yoga sanctuary. As soon as I turned on my iTunes to begin working on your photo album at the kitchen table, James Bay started playing. The song 'Incomplete' about 'pressing my lips down into your neck' brought to mind the times I would lie on top of you and gently kiss your neck and breathe you in deeply, and the times you would lie with your head on my chest and listen to my heart."

Here are the lyrics to this song.

"Incomplete" by James Bay

I breathe in slow to compose myself
But the bleeding heart I left on the shelf
Started speeding now, beating half to death
'Cause you're here and you're all mine

So I press my lips down into your neck
And I stay there and I reconnect
Bravery I've been trying to perfect
It can wait for a while

Scared of the hope in my head
It's been making me sweat, but it turns out
You're here with your head on my chest
I should have guessed

That the world will turn and we'll grow
We'll learn how to be
To be incomplete

I breathe out now and we fall back in
Just like before we can re-begin
Let your lungs push slow up against my skin
Let it all feel just right

Gone is the emptiness
We just take what's best and we move on
All of the hurt gets left
I should've guessed

That the world will turn and we'll grow
We'll learn how to be
To be incomplete
This, here, now
It's where we touch down
You and me
Let's be incomplete

How will we ever go without
I don't know
But it looks like we've made it again
Tell me you'll never look down, down
And the world will turn and we'll grow
We'll learn how to be
To be incom—

I don't wanna look down
I don't want us to break up in the clouds
All I want is to stay us, to stay with you now

I don't wanna look down
I don't want us to break up in the clouds
All I want is to stay us, to stay with you now

And the world will turn and we'll grow
We'll learn how to be
To be incomplete
And this, here, now
It's where we touch down
You and me
Let's be incomplete

July 14, 2019

Second Reading With Kay Fahlstrom, Via Phone

KAY: When I do first readings with someone, I do the protocol of letting the Spirit say whatever they want; getting 10 to 15 percent of the reading is proof that it's really Ann Marie. Today Ann Marie took charge and really started talking. And I was like, "Okay, clearly you're going to run the show today." And I'm like that's fine because Jenn knows that I can get proof and I've already done it. But she is just going to talk today.

ME: Okay. That's her running the show for sure [*laughing*].

KAY: She led me. So I'm just going to say that from the get-go. We are going to launch right in. You can just sit back and relax. I am glad you are recording this, right?

ME: Yes, I am.

KAY: She says, "Make no mistake, I'm going to come through loud and clear here today."

ME: Okay. Awesome. I asked her to.

KAY: I never hear that. I've never heard that in a reading—not once. She says, "Make no mistake, I'm going to be loud and clear." And I'm like, SWEET! She's funny today 'cause she's like, "Kay, forget about your questions. I'm just going to say what I want to say." Fine. You're running the show. Whatever you want to do. So today she's just going to run it.

She says, "I've been taking stock of things over here." Okay. She says, "There isn't enough time to tell you today how badly I feel … about so many things." So she's just saying, "You nurtured me, and I failed." You know. "You were there for me, and now I'm not there. It isn't fair." So she feels horrible about what she did.

ME: I know. I don't … I don't blame her. You know. I love her too much.

KAY: Right. And so that's beautiful because then she can heal and grow from that and then you can. Like, then you're both free. "Ahhhh!" [*Kay trying angelic singing*] Because then you're both free.

ME: Yeah. I mean, I miss her … I had planned on spending the rest of my life with her. It's scary for me over on this side of things … but that has nothing to do with her. I understand that we all have a path and maybe this was her path. And I don't … I don't place any blame with her. Of course, I wish it didn't happen, but you know, I'm not angry with her.

KAY: Okay. Beautiful. So it's very freeing. Freeing for you and her. But SHE needs to say some things still. "I'm so sorry about the ways that I hurt you." She says, "You're very strong to get through this." Ann Marie sees you making positive steps, and I know sometimes it's hard to just do things. But she says, "You're making a lot of positive steps." She says, "If the shoe were on the other foot … if it were you over here instead of me, and I was still there, I would be a wreck." You know. It would be super hard for her.

She's not saying it's easy for you, she's just saying, "WOW! I don't even know how you're doing it." She's full of admiration. She says, "I want you to keep hanging in there, please."

ME: Yes. Okay. It's not easy. Every minute of every day is … unbearable. I'm just faking it. Faking that I'm okay.

KAY: She says sometimes don't take a nosedive. Like there are times I'm sure when you want to just … I mean, it might just be a thought in your mind, and times when you're like ahhhh! It's hard to go on sometimes.

ME: Yeah. There are times. But most of the time, I try to stay positive and accept my sadness. And then there's times where my mind just goes, *Ahhhh! What am I doing here? I miss her and want to be with her.* Then I tell myself, *That's ridiculous. You have to be here.*

KAY: Right. Exactly. So she … you know, they know—sort of—our thoughts. They're not invading our privacy, but they know kind of what we're thinking at times. She changes topics a lot, which is very typical in a reading. But like, she'll say some things, and then the tone and mood might totally change. She's saying, "Your way of talking to me is so nice. The tones are kind." But she makes me feel like you're very kind and understanding and loving the way that you talk to her. She's showing you guys are in this space now where you are talking to each other a ton. Do you see that?

ME: Yeah. Most definitely.

KAY: Then she changes the topic or subject to just, like, an image.

ME: Yes.

KAY: You are both lying down together.

ME: Yes.

KAY: And your head is resting by her neck and shoulder. You're just kind of lying on her, you know.

ME: [*I am crying, having difficulty getting my words out.*] Yes. I just journaled about that last week.

KAY: And she's just showing that image with your head just under her chin, just resting on her chest. And it's very sweet. You journaled about that?

ME: [*I'm still crying.*] Yeah. Last week.

KAY: So that's her saying that she knows what's happening. Obviously, she knows you journaled about that, because it's rare for me to go into an image that's got no words with it. But it's just this peaceful, beautiful moment.

ME: Yeah. [*I'm trying to recover my composure.*]

KAY: Very good. Ann Marie says, "I visit you a lot, and I rock you and hold you when you're sad."

ME: Good. I feel her quite often, physically.

KAY: She's saying, "I do pop in and keep you company at work too."

ME: I do feel her a lot. And of course, I journal every day. And I always tell her that I love her. I end each page with "I love you, darling."

KAY: WOW. You know, if somebody were to write a book on how to heal, you'd be the perfect person. Because you're doing all the right things. It's beautiful what you just said. That's helping you so much. And it's a lovely tribute to her. A lot of people are stuck in their grief, and I feel like you are really working through it. But it doesn't mean your connection with her is going to go away. Okay?

ME: [*very softly*] Okay.

KAY: I asked Ann Marie, "Is there anything you want to talk about around that time period of when you crossed? Anything about how you were feeling? Do you want to say anything about it at all?" And some people in Spirit say, "NOPE" and move on. But she does want to say some things about this.

ME: Okay. Uh-huh.

KAY: This may overlap with some things she said before. She's saying something wasn't right in her mind. She would replay negative stuff in her mind that really bothered her. "I was wronged." Or "I feel bad that they did that to me as a child." Or "I feel bad that I didn't get this." It's like really old, old stuff that feels injurious to a kid. Okay. So it's like emotional impact. I feel like it was old. Like family stuff, or whatever experience that she had when she was younger.

ME: Was she in any kind of limbo or did she cross … did she transition … smoothly?

KAY: Ann Marie says, "I was received and taken over. I crossed over fully from the get-go." She wants to say, "I was stubborn and …"

ME: Yes.

KAY: She even uses the word (this is really kind of a powerful word) … She says, "Sometimes I was even belligerent."

ME: Yes.

KAY: Do you understand?

ME: Oh yes.

KAY: When we are on the Other Side, we look at our behavior. How we made other people feel. And she's been using this time on the Other Side. She visits you. She hangs out. But she's also been processing all these aspects about her personality and how it affected you and other people. She's saying, "Jenn, I was a part of your life. I wish it would have lasted longer."

ME: Yes, mmm. Me too.

KAY: So again, she changes the subject. Very typical in a reading. She says (it's fascinating the way she says this): "WE. WE. WEEEE … parade around you with our love." It's almost like weaving blankets of love around you. Isn't that beautiful? WE is more than her. So there is more than just Ann Marie working on trying to send you healing. Beautiful.

ME: [*quietly*] Yeah.

KAY: Then she gets all passionate. "YOU ROCKED MY WORLD!"

ME: Oh my gosh [*laughing*].

KAY: Like "WHOOOOA! A love I had never felt before."

ME: Yeah. She told me that, and I told her that too. Yeah. Definitely.

KAY: She's talking about the alignment. "We got each other. We were just aligned." Big, huge, massive love.

ME: Yeah. Yeah.

KAY: Like "A love I've never felt before." She goes, "Why did I screw it up?" And she says, "I'm ashamed I'll tell you that." So she can't not say this because she's going through the processing of it there.

ME: [*softly*] Yeah.

KAY: She says, "I feel like I'm never going to get over this, but they assure me here that I can and I will."

So it's like there's these warm, friendly, counselor kind of people there. And it's not like going to therapy. It's not like you have to go to therapy in Heaven. It's more like these kind, sweet people checking in with you and helping you see it in another way. She's got help there.

ME: Good.

KAY: I asked Ann Marie, "How do you come through to Jenn?" She says, "At night." She really likes nighttime, but she visits during the day and at work and stuff too. She says she whispers words in your ear.

ME: Okay.

KAY: And so, you know, it's hard for you to hear, but do you get the sense of when she's around you?

ME: I do. I feel a lot of it comes through music. It's really weird. I don't know if she's getting better at it, but she's definitely trying to express how she felt/feels through songs. When I journaled last week, I wrote about a song I felt she had sent me. It was by James Bay, and he sings, "I bury my lips into your neck." I used to do that all the time with Ann Marie. And her with me. She would listen to my heart.

KAY: Yeah, and that's the image she showed earlier.

ME: [*softly*] Yeah.

KAY: Your face is in her neck. She whispers in your ear, "I'm home, baby." Music. There are songs about "you stole my heart"—but in a good way. You know, like "I have a crush on you." All manner of love songs.

ME: Yeah. Yeah.

KAY: And then why is she saying a number? I can't quite make it out—like 17? Or 7? Does that mean anything to you?

ME: 17 or 7? I'm dyslexic, so bear with me, please. [*pause*] No, no idea.

[*Follow-up: I was at our neighbor's condo (who lived upstairs and across from Ann Marie and me) so I could use her landline while recording my reading with my cell phone. Her unit was #17. I was unaware of the number until I saw it as I exited the condominium.*]

KAY: And it's so easy to express herself through music. She's hilarious. She is saying she still touches you. She says she pinches your butt [*laughing*]. And she gives you tender touches too. Hugging. Softly brushing the back of your hair. Do you ever feel, sense her around you like that?

ME: It's only been the last two weeks. And I was like, *Did I just feel that?* One was like on my ear. Another was on my face in the middle of the night. I was intrigued, excited, and confused all at the same time. Yeah. I mean I feel it. But then, of course, I questioned, *Did I really feel that?*

KAY: Yeah. They can actually do that.

ME: Yeah. No, and that was one of the questions I had for you, because I kind of felt I was like losing it a little bit. I'm like, *Wait, was that ...? Is that possible?*

KAY: Yup. And I know how weird that feels. It takes them a lot of energy to do that. Like, she is telling me she's touching you, and that's a rare thing for me to hear. Okay.

ME: Okay.

KAY: She says there's something about the wind or the breeze. And she can get something across that way or get your attention.

ME: YES! YES!

KAY: Well, maybe it's a breezy day, and somehow it's affecting you. Maybe it's a still day, but then there's a breeze.

ME: Exactly. Yup. It happened last night, and it happens like when it will be still, and then a breeze will pick up, and I just instantly get this feeling—that's Ann Marie and God and the universe. It's everything and it's right there. They are kind of wrapping their love around me.

KAY: That's exactly the thing. I love it. That's beautiful. She says, "Nature." When you're out in nature, because you're at a higher vibration then. And music … perfect … because we get into a higher vibration with music also.

She says something about the cycles of nature. You know—spring, summer, fall, winter. With the cycles of nature, this will get better. Less difficult for you. It's hard to believe now, but it will. So it's almost like marking the improvement of the grief over the seasons of the year.

ME: Okay. I can't imagine ever feeling better.

KAY: She's showing me she gets your attention with flying animals. Butterflies. Dragonflies. Hummingbirds. But the butterflies are a favorite sign to send you. She's made me see at least five while I was meditating.

She's saying something more about music. Music. Music. Music. Music. Is one of your girls into music? Or going to study music?

ME: Yeah. They both started piano lessons. I'm going to Costco to buy a piano today. Ann Marie would not allow us to buy a piano because the noise would be overwhelming for her.

KAY: Oh, how beautiful that she knows about that. She's good when she takes over the reading. She says whatever it is she wants to say. I'm her humble servant. And she still gets the evidence in there.

ME: Yeah. Oh gosh, so much.

KAY: She's good. I said, "Tell me something about you." And she says, "I was a shooting star. A bright flame that shot across the sky. With a shorter life span." She says (it's interesting how she describes this): "I loved us together. You and me together. Like, there we are." I don't know how even to say it. Like "We're squished together like an Oreo.

So much so that it must be harder to have me here. I'm sorry. We were so together that this must be hard for you."

ME: Yeah. Exactly. She and the girls are my everything.

KAY: She says, "You're right next to me a lot. So don't feel like you're alone." So she's visiting A LOT. And yeah, there is something about the house that you are living in. I said, "Show me something that you can see." Were you thinking about changing it? Or renovating something?

ME: YES!

KAY: Okay. She's saying … Is it okay if Ann Marie gives her two cents?

ME: Yes.

KAY: She's saying, "Oh, it's fine the way it is. You don't have to do more. Save your money."

ME: Oh shit. She always was like that. Oh gawd. I already started. I killed the front lawn. I'm replacing the front lawn. It's costing me $900, with labor and everything.

KAY: [*Laughing*]

ME: So it's too late now. Sorry. I gotta replace it. I sprayed it with Roundup!

KAY: You're the perfect person to fix it. She's saying, "You don't have to spend more money. It's okay the way it is." But you have 100 percent free will. That is something she sees going on.

So this reading is different from the first. She needed to share different things today. There may be some overlap. But what was it like to hear from her today?

ME: Oh amazing. The breeze. The touching. The image of us and how I just journaled about that. Those are all things I have felt so strongly. You had mentioned the music. The stubbornness. I mean, totally. Her stubbornness was difficult to deal with at times. I still loved her anyway. I loved her so much.

KAY: Mmm, and still do. But she's around you a lot. She is wrapped up a lot in processing it and visiting you. She really needs to say her stuff, even though you are really gracious toward her, so that you can both heal.

July 20, 2019

She's Giving Me Strength Through Music

As I mentioned, Ann Marie sent me oodles of songs to communicate her love for me, how she felt while here, and how she feels now. Yes, I do believe, even beyond death, that Ann Marie still has consciousness. Her desires. Her wishes. Her mistakes. Any and all sorts of thoughts and feelings. Many of the songs she's sent me I had never heard before.

I was having a rougher day than usual dealing with accusations and rumors from certain groups of people down south. I had been receiving random text messages and information through the grapevine with horrible and despicable rumors about my apparent involvement in Ann Marie's death. I was terribly distraught, to say the very least. This song came through on July 20, directly after I received an unscrupulous text message.

"Be Here Now" by Ray LaMontagne

Don't let your mind get weary and confused
Your will be still, don't try…
Don't let your heart get heavy
Child, inside you, there's a strength that lies

Don't let your soul get lonely
Child, it's only time, it will go by
Don't look for love in faces, places
It's in you that's where you'll find…

Kindness
Be.

Be here now, be here now
Be…
Be here now, be here now
Don't lose your faith in me

And I will try not to lose faith in you
Don't put your trust in walls
'Cause walls will only crush you when they fall
Be…
Be here now, be here now
Be…
Be here now, be here now
Be here now, be here now

Ann Marie sent me this song to give me strength. To tell me not to listen to what people were saying and the gossip that was swirling around. To look inside myself, so I would find power and strength deep within my Soul.

At this point, Ann Marie and I were communicating a lot. "Be here now" for us means to simply be with her and let all the outside chatter go.

I guess when something so awful and horrific happens like Ann Marie's death, people need to make sense of it. Someone so young, so beautiful, so intelligent, so funny, and full of so much life. It was easiest to point their fingers at me. Implicating me made sense to many for something they could not make sense of. It doesn't hurt me any longer, and my best path to peace within myself is total forgiveness of others' cruelties.

August 8, 2019

She's In The Wind

Many times, up until this day, I could sense Ann Marie in the breeze. It was everything—Ann Marie and the universe. Unless you have felt it yourself, it is difficult to describe. It's an overwhelming feeling of love and peace. I had never experienced this until Ann Marie's passing. I journaled about it, but never told a soul what I had experienced.

Honestly, I was a little embarrassed to share it with anyone.

On this day in August, the girls and I stepped out the front door and sat on the top step of our porch to put our shoes on. The girls had slip-on shoes, whereas I had to tie my laces. As I sat there tying and the girls stood to wait for me, Ella exclaimed with sheer delight, "There's Ann Marie!!"

Shocked and confused, I looked up and down the street and asked, "Where, honey?" I couldn't help the small glimmer of hope that I would see Ann Marie walking up the sidewalk to our home.

It sounds strange, but I had been having a lot of dreams about Ann Marie still being alive and well. In my dreams I could clearly see her—while everyone else could not. Often I would exclaim to the other people in my dreams "She is right there! Can't you see her? She is sitting in that chair—why can't you see her?" So a part of my subconscious was grappling with her loss. There were many days when the thought of Ann Marie being gone was inconceivable—like it was just a bad nightmare.

Ella replied, "The wind!"

I asked, "Why do you say that, sweetie?"

"Because God is wind and everywhere."

This feeling I had been experiencing was shared by a six-and-a-half-year-old. I always felt as if it was God and Ann Marie. Ella felt this as well. A Soul so young, who really had no idea about what had been lost was feeling Ann Marie the way I had.

For me, this was validation that I was not imagining what I had felt. Out of the mouths of babes.

August 20, 2019

Kindred Souls

Ann Marie and I worked together the last year of her life. She had been experiencing burnout and stress at her work and wanted a job that was less stressful. She mentioned several times to me that she should get a job at Trader Joe's stocking shelves. She just wanted something mindless and stress-free. I offered to let her come work with me. I could pay her more than Trader Joe's could, we would be together, I would have some company, and it would be fun. She would be outdoors seeing nature and the sky instead of cooped up in an office all day.

She loved nature. When we first met, we were walking through the park and stopped at the same time, to watch two butterflies do an eloquent dance. We got so much joy out of that. Something so sweet and simple. That's when I realized, *Wow, kindred Souls*. I'll never forget that.

Well, she took me up on the offer. We had so much fun together. We would laugh with my crew and enjoy the days. She was an excellent student. I showed her how to prune roses and hydrangeas, perennials, and evergreen shrubs. (All our pruning is done by hand, no gas trimmers. The clients love that, and I wouldn't have it any other way.) She got attacked by a yellow jacket at a maintenance account, and I fiercely swatted it away and repeatedly stepped on it. Sorry, little guy, but ain't no wasp going to attack my woman. One time, my employee Ivan tossed a banana slug at her, and I can still hear the scream she let out. Jose placed a small plastic toy turtle in a garden, and I can still hear her voice when she found it and thought it was real for a moment. She squealed with delight. We all laughed a lot.

Another time we were at Marcy's, her favorite client, and Ann Marie inadvertently squirted me in the face with the hose as she untangled it. She thought it was quite amusing. I was angry, but as soon as I saw her laughing and getting such pleasure out of beaming me in the face with a hard squirt of water, I couldn't help but laugh myself.

Marcy's garden holds a lot of memories for me. All wonderful and amazing. This is the same client who pointed me in the direction of our condominium deed.

It is not often I listen to music with lyrics, but occasionally at Marcy's and a few other garden maintenance accounts, I put my iTunes on shuffle. I say a prayer and invite Ann Marie to be with me. I wear my headset and listen to music while I do detailed pruning. Talk about a low-stress job—it's wonderful. Ann Marie has sent me some meaningful songs this way. Most I have never heard before. Here is one of them. In fact, I don't even know how it ended up in my iTunes library.

"This Ain't Goodbye" by Train

You and I were friends from outer space
Afraid to let go
The only two who understood this place
And as far as we know
We were way before our time

As bold as we were blind
Just another perfect mistake
Another bridge to take
On the way to letting go

This ain't goodbye
It is just the way love goes
When the words aren't warm enough,
To keep away the cold, oh no
This ain't goodbye
It's not where our story ends
But I know you can't be mine,
Not the way you've always been
As long as we've got time
Then this ain't goodbye
Oh no, this ain't goodbye

We were stars up in the sunlit sky
No one else could see
Neither of us ever thought to ever ask why
It wasn't meant to be
Maybe we were way too high
To ever understand
Baby, we were victims of all, all the foolish plans
We began to divide

But this ain't goodbye
This is just the way love goes
When words aren't warm enough
To keep away the cold, oh no
This ain't goodbye

It's not where our story ends
But I know you can't be mine
Not the way you've always been
As long as we've got time,
This ain't goodbye
Oh no, this ain't goodbye

You and I were friends from outer space
Afraid to let go
The only two who understood this place

And as far as we know
This ain't goodbye
Oh no, this ain't goodbye
This ain't goodbye
Oh no, this ain't goodbye
This ain't goodbye
This is just the way our love goes
When the words aren't warm enough,
To keep away the cold, oh no
This ain't goodbye
It's not where our story ends
But I know you can't be mine
Not the way you've always been
Oh no, don't say it

Don't say goodbye

September 3, 2019

Second Reading With Jeanne Leto, Via Phone

Roni, a longtime friend of mine, was staying with me on the nights I did not have the children to keep me company. She had a heavy, negative sensation of Ann Marie's presence in the room she was sleeping in. Roni and I decided to reach out to Jeanne to help communicate to Ann Marie that she was in the home to help me navigate the nights, which early on were very scary for me.

For the first year or more, the lights on the upstairs floor flickered frequently, and at night the floors creaked and cracked as if someone was walking around. The first two years after Ann Marie's passing, the house—especially our bedroom—was teeming with noises and energy.

Today, the house is completely silent … no more flickering lights and no more footsteps on the stairs, hallway, or bedrooms.

JEANNE: I have an energy here. I have Ann Marie, but it's very … I'll be honest with you—she said Martha. She's upset about Martha.

ME: Okay. That's Ann Marie's mom.

JEANNE: And I want to ask you another question before I pray … I don't know who David and Jose were. I don't know if she's bilingual or something, because I feel the name Martha is very Hispanic, so she has … I almost feel like she had two languages or two selves. And it's almost like when she came through before—it was like frantic, and it's not frantic anymore, because I feel more peaceful energy connected to her.

This woman … I picked up that there was something that happened with the police, but I don't feel it was the first time. I definitely feel that she had problems with a license or something. I feel she was a tormented Soul for a couple years, honey. I feel like she finally has peace. I think you really need to know that she is finally at peace. She was tormented about things.

Do you understand what I'm feeling from her?

ME: I do. I do. And she was bilingual. She worked with me for the last nine months, and she helped me out with the guys a lot. She spoke to them in Spanish.

JEANNE: Okay. Fine. But she's very brilliant. Like, I feel very fluent. Very fluent energy.

ME: Oh yes. I really admired that about her.

JEANNE: Well, she was no dummy. This girl was absolutely no dummy. But it was her anger and rage from abuse. I feel that she felt you were very kind, and I'm gonna stick with how she's making me feel, because I'm seeing a big heart, and I literally was asked to get the butterfly cards to start out the reading.

I'm gonna pray because she's, like, throwing things at me … like, there's a V initial. She's pointing to somebody with a V. So I don't know if she knew anybody with a V initial that was very strongly connected to her. She's talking about a Carlos as well. So I mean, you know, going all over the board with her. So I need to say a prayer.

ME: Okay.

JEANNE: I need your friend's birthday as well.

ME: What's your birthday, Roni?

RONI: June 6, 1961.

JEANNE: Okay. Perfect. I honor everyone's belief systems. I do have a strong faith in God. But I just ask from my heart. Please, Heavenly Father, help me to be a blessing to these women. I do ask specifically now, Archangels Michael and Rafael, please come. I ask for a circle of light around everyone. I pray from every cell of my being that this is a blessing. Thank you, Father. Amen and amen and amen.

ME: Amen.

JEANNE: I'm gonna call her Ann or Annie. The only energy I am allowing to come through is Ann Marie with the brown shoulder-length hair, and I guess that's who you want. She's talking about bruises. Who got bruises? What happened? Who got bruises?

ME: Like right now? Or …?

JEANNE: I don't know, but she's talking about bruises.

ME: Um …

RONI: I don't know.

ME: Um … I don't know …

JEANNE: She's talking about somebody having bruises. Ann Marie is. So unless there were a bunch of bruises on her neck?

ME: I didn't see her. I mean I saw her, but I didn't look.

JEANNE: Okay. I'm gonna stick with it 'cause she's talking about bruises and her neck.

ME: [*I speak slowly, drawing out the syllables of my response, as I ponder the image of her bruises and what Ann Marie may be trying to say.*] Okayyy … she could have …

JEANNE: So what did she actually end up doing to herself?

ME: She hung herself.

JEANNE: That's what it is. Okay. That's what she's talking about. All the bruises on her neck.

ME: Okay. Um … she … I don't want to know. Never mind.

JEANNE: Okay. She's making me feel she's gone through the whole thing about her neck, and I feel she's got a real different energy connected with Roni, and I don't understand why. Why doesn't Roni ask her a question?

RONI: I just want to know if … because when I'm here I feel very unsettled and at night I can't sleep. Jennifer and I are best friends.

JEANNE: Okay. Well, all of a sudden, I feel very unsettled that Roni is there. And I feel, like, very kind of aggressive. And she's now making me feel about her neck, which we didn't discuss before. I knew that somehow something happened with the police, and all of a sudden, she's very unsettled. And very kind of … a little bit aggressive [*uncomfortable laugh*].

ME: Can we let her know that Roni is just here keeping me company at nighttime?

JEANNE: I think Roni already knows that she is bothering her. Let me talk to her and see what I can do.

Please help me to communicate this. You need to understand, Ann Marie, that I don't like how you're feeling aggressive and making me feel. Please give me your feelings about why you're so upset about Roni being there. I just want to know the truth. And I will be honest and relay this to the girls.

Okay. I'm going to ask, and I want you to use my cards. Let's just ask her why. And you know I get more pictures with my cards. I'm just gonna ask why. All right?

ME: Okay. Okay.

JEANNE: Okay. Heartbreak. I'm watching from Heaven. Um …

ME: Okay.

JEANNE: Soulmate. Ohhh … okay so … yes she's not happy about it. I think she feels uncomfortable. I'm not gonna lie. It does actually show it. I see her kind of battling with … Obviously she can't come in all the time because there's a veil—the woman feels threatened. I can see it.

Five of Cups. Eight of Swords and … here's your girl, Ann Marie. She's coming in as the Queen of Coins, and it's jealousy. She's around watching her like a damn dog.

ME: Yeah, I know, but we are just friends.

JEANNE: She's watching her like a damn dog. That's the only way I can tell you from looking at these cards, and it makes me uncomfortable for Roni.

ME: There is no ... there is no ... nothing.

RONI: We're just friends. We've only been just friends for like 20 years.

JEANNE: Look, in her mind, even though she made it to the Other Side, thank God. She's not physically there, like stuck every day hanging herself—which I didn't know was the cause of her death. I just knew she was dead. Now it's like, thank God she's made it across, but it's like she keeps coming back. Like she's tormented. TORMENTED. She's jealous. We take our feelings over there, honey.

ME: BUT ... [*sighing*]

JEANNE: And you're just going to have to explain to her. I'm explaining to her. I feel she's possessive, and that's kind of why she is not letting your friend sleep. And I feel sorry for your friend.

RONI: I'm very uncomfortable here. At night she's, like, in my room. Jenn said she could hear her in there too.

JEANNE: I'm seeing it, honey.

RONI: Remember, like, footsteps?

JEANNE: Roni, I'm getting a chill and she is touching me. It's like "Yeah. Uh-huh. I'm watching you." No matter what, she was very jealous. She had a short fuse—nobody can tell me any different because she had a short fuse. And she is watching Roni.

ME: [*softly*] Okay.

JEANNE: Territory. I'm sorry. The only word I can use is *territory*.

RONI: So can we communicate to her that I'm just here to support?

JEANNE: This is terrible.

ME: Oooo!

JEANNE: I feel sorry for your friend. Okay—she is not going to stop. I just heard that. And I mean that from my heart. She can't help herself. Like, um, 'cause she's so tied into you, Jenn. I'm sorry. She's so tied into you and the children and the place where she crossed. I mean, she's very tied into that energy.

ME: Yeah. Okay.

JEANNE: You're like her doll. You're, like, pure. You were kind. These are the energies she's making me feel. You were a breath of fresh air to her. She had a bit of a toxic lifestyle. I feel like she was an intelligent person. Probably a very learned person. I feel like academically she was very learned.

ME: Yes.

JEANNE: I do feel like she was more connected to toxicity. Does that make sense? And I'm saying this in front of her. I'm not hiding it.

ME: Yeah … yeah … yeah.

JEANNE: And you were pure to her. Do you understand? It's like she's aggressively watching your friend. [*in a low tone*] It's not cool.

ME: What did you say?

JEANNE: It's not cool. Can you sage or whatever? I'm sorry, I'm gonna tell them if you don't behave yourself, I will tell them how. Do you sage? Sage that room every day so she can't stay in that room.

RONI: Well, no. Does that help?

JEANNE: Please sage. Please, it will. She won't be able … She's a little pissed, I'm telling you. She won't be able to stand the smoke. White sage. Do it in the corners. She'll be in that house, but she won't be in that room with you. It will calm it down. She's a little annoyed at me for saying that, but she can watch from another vantage point. She is watching. I just want to go into the bathroom and see her. Like, all of a sudden, "I think I saw her in a mirror—was that her?" and a lightbulb kind of went off or a TV flickering. I'm just seeing shit like that happen.

RONI: Oh, the lights were flickering the other night in that room. Remember the lights flickering?

ME: Yes. We knew it was her.

JEANNE: That's her.

RONI: I was upstairs the other night, and the lights upstairs started flickering A LOT.

JEANNE: It's her!

RONI: I can feel it.

JEANNE: She's letting you know she's around, and it's territory and she wants you to stay away from her. It's kind of like "I'm the beast, I'll turn into a beast" kind of deal.

She had a temper, this girl. I mean, she was a live wire. Nobody can tell me any different. I swear to God I picked up on an arrest, but I feel like there might have been a couple arrests with her on DUIs. She's had trouble.

ME: Was she around me today? Because …

JEANNE: She's around—when you're around, she's around ALL the time. I feel like she's haunted. She's tormented. When I read you before and I was very sweet and I felt … the anger and the rage at first, at herself. She was saying, "I was mad at myself." Now it's just like, "Challenge me. I might be in the Spirit world, but I have the upper hand" type of deal.

ME: [*nervously*] Okay.

RONI: JESUS!

ME: Shh … please don't say Jesus's name in vain.

JEANNE: I don't like how this reading has gone. I'm very uncomfortable. Can we ask some other questions and stuff?

ME: Yeah. Yeah.

JEANNE: I'm definitely very upset. I definitely would want to acknowledge somebody with the V initial. So I don't know why she keeps putting a V in front of me. Who has the V initial that she loved?

ME: Oh!! Valerie, my mom. Valerie!

JEANNE: There you go! Okay. There you go.

ME: She liked my mom a lot. [*I'm relieved to have a new topic.*]

JEANNE: Let's switch over to that 'cause I feel like with you two … I said, "I have to stop this," 'cause I feel like she's like a dog on a bone. Let's go with Mom's energy. When she put the V in front of me, I felt warmth. That was a sign to me that she was really very grateful for how kind your mother is.

ME: Yeah. Yeah. My mom is really sweet, and we used to go up to my parents' vineyard, and we had a lot of wonderful times up there. Ann Marie loved to be outdoors helping my dad, who's 88 years old, helping him on the vineyard and mowing the fields. She liked to do that, and it was, I think, a place where she could just be in nature. She loved nature. We both do. One time she almost rolled the tractor—that was scary. [*I'm happy to elaborate on a different topic.*]

JEANNE: She liked the family atmosphere. I heard "family." I heard the words "family" and "warmth." And I feel that is why she fell for you. There's a warmth to you and a kindness (now she's calming down) that attracted her. I feel like she had some rough goes in her life, man.

ME: I know. I know she did. She told me about them.

JEANNE: I just feel like the abuse, sexual abuse. Somebody hurt her more than once, connected to her family. I just feel like you … that was a cocoon for her. I just want to bring her to another level. 'Cause I don't like what I was feeling. Because I was taking on her energy.

ME: Is she able to …?

JEANNE: She can manipulate things at this point.

ME: Like birds and stuff?

JEANNE: Absolutely. They are heavenly signs from loved ones who have crossed. She has been picking on your friend. She isn't letting her sleep.

ME: I've got sage. We'll sage today.

JEANNE: Sage the shit out of that room [*laughing*].

ME: [*Laughing*]

JEANNE: Oh my God. I'm sorry. I'm sorry. I hate to do that to a Spirit, but when she's not playing fair ball with your friend … I can tell you right now, besides the lights flickering—I'm gonna tell you right now, your friend's gonna see her out of the corner of her eye.

RONI: I already have!

JEANNE: Because she's shown me—full manifestation of her. Like, it's in color. Okay. She's good at doing this already. She's good at it. I'm telling you, this girl is powerful. She knows how to manipulate energy. She's laughing. I, all of a sudden, see her laughing. She's getting a kick out of some of the stuff she's doing, which is not really cool. I've never dealt with anyone like her, to be honest, Jenn. I mean … I like her, but she scares me a little bit.

ME: OH GREAT! [*Laughing*]

JEANNE & RONI: [*Laughing*]

ME: Great!

JEANNE: Do you own a place with her? She feels like she owns something with you. She's saying, "I got a contract—with Jenn." That you guys might have a contract on a home together.

ME: We own a condo together.

JEANNE: She feels she owns something with you. "I own that. I own it with her. I have something with her." She feels like she has some sort of contract with you. I don't think this woman is ready to let you go. And I feel like it will take like a Mother Teresa for her to approve of someone for you. 'Cause I'm telling you, I don't think she likes Roni.

ME: Okay.

JEANNE: It's not like Roni is a bad person. The problem is, she's jealous.

ME: Yeah. She had a very strong jealous side.

JEANNE: No SHIT!

[All three of us are laughing together now.]

JEANNE: This is a little fucked up. I've never dealt with a Spirit that's this, um, tormented. She's got a little cray-cray going on with her. She's pretty, but she got a little cray-cray goin' on with her. She was a handful.

ME: I know she is. But does she have people over there helping her, like working through …?

JEANNE: I feel like when we started to get into the reading last time, I started to get really—like, "Holy shit!"—angry. And I feel like when she goes into subjects that she likes, she's fine, she's wonderful. But when something escalates her, this girl is off the charts.

ME: Yeah.

JEANNE: I feel like she had a jealousy with Roni when she was alive.

ME: Yes.

JEANNE: So why would she be any different now, is kind of what I'm asking you.

ME: Yeah.

JEANNE: It's just. It's—whoever it is—we take our personality with us over there. She has something against Roni, is what the cards are showing. That she had it when she was here. And why wouldn't she be jealous now? And she's jealous of the children a little bit. Sorry. You know that to be true, right?

ME: Yeah. I did. She wrote me a letter about a week before she died. She touched on that a little bit. She didn't understand her feelings of jealousy toward the children.

JEANNE: She's been through IT!

ME: Yeah.

JEANNE: I don't know why she is taking me out to Hawaii. I don't know if anyone had made any plans about Hawaii, but she is showing me Hawaii.

ME: I journaled about that a week ago. My brother-in-law's parents have a condominium there. There's a little church on the beach next to the condominium, and that's where I always fantasized that we would have a commitment ceremony.

JEANNE: That's in Hawaii? Okay, 'cause she's taking me out there. I actually did get her to laugh. I can see her laughing. Thank God, because I'm like ready to karate chop somebody. I'm like ready to kick anybody that gets in my way. She must have been a little wild one, holy shit balls.

RONI: She was a handful.

JEANNE: Holy shit [*laughing*]. Thank God she had a good sense of humor, because I tell you that's probably the only thing that stopped her from doing this even when she was younger. I feel like she's had three … Okay, she's channeling me now. She's had three close calls.

ME: Yes.

JEANNE: Where she's come close to killing herself before. You know that, right?

ME: Yes. She called it the "Ring of Fire." She said she survived it and it would never, ever be an option again.

JEANNE: She would have done it anyway because all the emotions that I feel after this … going through. She had so many emotions. She had many of her own demons. But I can tell you she does love you, and I can tell you right now that unfortunately there is an ownership problem here and feeling that she wants to go to Hawaii and get married now. But she can't. But she still wants to. She will pick that right person for you, but she's not ready right now.

RONI: [*Laughing*]

JEANNE: It is what it is. She'll "find the right person for you" is what she said [*laughing*].

RONI: So she's controlling here and she's controlling in the afterlife.

JEANNE: You can't make this shit up. I don't know who was from New York, or somebody connected to New York, why she's talking about something about New York. I don't know who was in New York or a connection there.

ME: She was born there. In Trenton.

JEANNE: There you go. I didn't know. So there you go. I haven't even been drinking, but I feel like driving up and getting a big bottle of red wine right now. I swear … God … holy shit!

[*We're all laughing together again.*]

October 5, 2019

Second Reading With Sandra O'Hara, In Person
Mill Valley, California

SANDRA: Now, you may think you've already been on a massive learning curve, and in fairness you have, but it is continuing. The learning that's coming is more of your physical learning. Like reading and experiencing things. But there is a creative aspect to you that's wanting to come out, you know? And when it's out, it's not going back in again.

ME: Okay.

SANDRA: But it's also going to be something you will share with others around you. Whether that's like family and friends or it's a wide circle.

ME: Okay.

SANDRA: She tells me she couldn't cope. She had a lot of voices in her head. See the Ganesh statue over there with different heads? [*She points to Ganesh.*]

ME: [*I turn in my seat to look behind me.*] Yes.

SANDRA: She said, "That was me." Like, she had these heads. Do you know what I mean? That would argue with each other. Highly, highly intelligent woman. It's not like she's blaming her upbringing. She's not. But she is saying she didn't get the best start in life. She said she had to do a lot of work on herself where anger management was concerned. But she couldn't always keep the lid on it. She also would cuss. Like, bad language straight out of her. I think she felt she had a demon in her. Do you know what I mean?

ME: She told me, "Jenn, I'm so broken." And I knew that when she would be horrible to me that it wasn't her. She didn't mean it.

SANDRA: And that's part of the message today. There's almost like a gratefulness from her to you. That you gave her a semblance of a normal life. Don't dwell on the words "a semblance of." Do you know what I mean? This was more than any normality she had in her life previously. She does say that you were exceptionally patient, and you forgave her a lot of stuff that other people would not forgive. It's something she had attempted before—taking her life—previous to meeting you.

And she's also very sorry for the way she was found. She knows that was traumatic and will always be traumatic. She is telling me that she had a psychotic break at the end. It's like, if you take the brake off the car going downhill, it's going to gather speed. Do you know what I mean? "I just sometimes forgot to put my foot on the brake to stop it from gathering speed."

There is a side of her that is exceptionally compassionate, that would do anything for anybody. You know? But when that darkness came in, you wouldn't have a torch bright enough to shed light on it. Do you know what I am saying? When we pass to Spirit, it's not that we suddenly grow wings and become angels; we don't. But we do get to see ourselves as we truly are, and we also see others as they are, and what we need and what they need. You and Ann Marie are twin flames, in my opinion.

They are the ones you've had karmic lifetimes with. Do you know what I mean?

ME: Yes.

SANDRA: And that you were meant to be together in this life and happily so, although it was a sad ending. What I do feel with her, though, is that she would have brought a lot of volatility to your life. But I think you were the correct person for that, in that you had the patience and the ability to center yourself and ground yourself. And she's saying, "Nobody else would have put up with me."

ME: Mm-hm.

SANDRA: Because she would have been very exacting and very demanding. Now this is her life personality she is bringing through. This is not how she is now in Spirit.

ME: Mm-hm.

SANDRA: She's showing me an unborn baby with her as well. So I don't know whether she lost a baby—like a miscarriage or a termination or a stillbirth.

ME: Termination.

SANDRA: So she has an unborn baby. Well, it's born in Spirit. Not born here. It would be her baby.

ME: Yes.

SANDRA: She tells me she is content in Spirit. And she shows me, she likes the sunlight on water. The way it would sparkle on water. Also, she keeps pointing to her feet. And she's barefoot. Does that make any sense to you?

ME: She was really beautiful. Everything about her was perfect. But she did have an operation on both feet at the joint of the large toe.

SANDRA: Right. Okay. Well, she's showing me her feet, and they are beautiful, and she is barefoot. Like, "Look at my feet. Aren't they lovely?"

ME: I think that was the only thing she didn't like about her body.

SANDRA: She's showing me, and they are beautiful. She's admiring her feet. And they are bare, on the ground. She's like, "I am so much more grounded here." She kind of winked then, and she's gonna catch you next time around. You've got a karmic connection. Your Souls will know each other. She's promising that. Did she play with your hair a lot? She's playing with my hair.

ME: She didn't. But she does a lot of things. I swear last week I think she pinched my nose to wake me up in the middle of the night. It was abrupt and hard. Can she touch me?

SANDRA: Oh yeah. They can. They can manifest that. She hasn't left you, you know. She hasn't left you. That doesn't mean she's not fully participating in what she needs to participate in, in Spirit. It's her love for you that keeps her around you. Because you need that right now.

Did she have a bit of a fender bender? She's showing me a bit of damage to a vehicle.

ME: Well, she got into an accident the day before she died.

SANDRA: Okay. She says that was completely her fault. Like, she tells me she was high.

ME: Yeah.

SANDRA: Like, that's the word. "I was high." And she's showing me, like, a fender bender. She was on a warning as well. With someone or someplace. Was she still working?

ME: She was working with me in the garden. She took a leave of absence.

SANDRA: Oh. Okay.

ME: She worked at JumpstartMD. She was the clinic manager. They wanted her to run all of Northern California, but she didn't want that kind of stress. She had done that before working for Lindora in Southern California.

SANDRA: Okay. Had she gotten a warning there? Or had she gotten a reprimand of some sort at JumpstartMD?

ME: Yes. She didn't like it. She got into an argument with the owner in front of the staff at the office, and that's what caused a lot of stress for her at work. Going into work after that was very hard for her. I think she was extremely embarrassed.

SANDRA: Yeah, yeah, because she's showing a reprimand—but like this fender bender, it was "just one more thing I couldn't take," is what she says. It was like a whole culmination of things that led her to taking her life, of which you are not one of them.

Although, she does tell me (and she laughs when she's saying it) you spoke in what you thought was a harsh way to her. Do you know what

I mean? She said, "Oh my gawd, I've been so much harsher with you, and yet you have convinced yourself that that is why I did what I did." So does that make sense?

ME: Mm-hm. I—

SANDRA: So she's saying, "NO."

ME: I play over in my head some things that I said the night she passed. I mean, they weren't that bad, and I didn't even mean them, but I just feel so bad for saying them. I was so angry and confused toward the end of her life. She had several bad episodes that threw me for a loop. I didn't know how to handle the situation. I was worried about the kids, so very worried about protecting the kids. I went into mother-bear mode.

SANDRA: I know. I know. And so, you've been giving yourself a hard time and you've been believing on some level that the things that you said contributed to what she did or the actions that she chose to take. You know it's not that she's laughing at you—like funny, ha-ha—but she's like, "Oh my gawd, I said things so much worse to you, and trust me, what you said to me was well deserved and more. I am the reason I did what I did."

The fender bender was like the straw that broke the camel's back with her.

You brought sunshine into her life, as did your girls.

Is one of your girls having some issues to do with the tummy area or like the womb—the ovaries—something like that?

ME: Ah, Nisa had an operation on her … one of the ovaries didn't drop or something … I can't remember exactly what the condition was. She was born with it.

SANDRA: But, like, did Ann Marie help her with that? Or help you with that?

ME: Yes. Ann Marie was there.

SANDRA: But it was like the one time she thought she could do something for you, you know, on a parenting level with your girls. That … that was like, she felt "There's a future here. There's a family here." And then (excuse my expression), she says, "I had to go and fuck it up."

ME: [*quietly*] Yeah.

SANDRA: She's also talking to me about playing with the lights, with the electric. She says, "I do that quite a lot."

ME: I talk to the light, and it answers. They flicker a lot. And then she does stuff on my computer and my phone. I told the computer guy, "All these files that were Ann Marie's, they just changed one week after she passed away to PDF files. They were in Word. Then just all of a sudden, changed."

He said, "That's impossible."

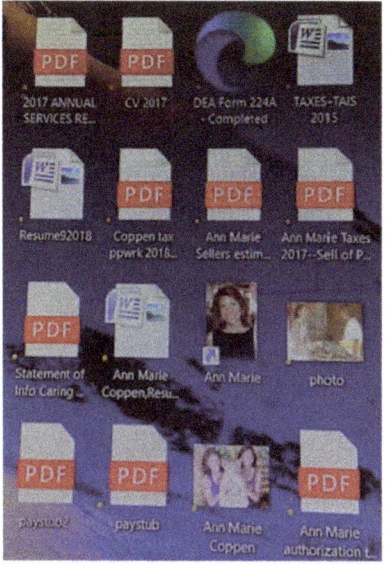

SANDRA: As far as the computer doing it, it's impossible, but *she* did it. She's trying to communicate with you, you know, and she's a very strong character.

ME: Yes. She sure is and was.

SANDRA: To the point of being bloody-minded. Do you know what I mean? She's like, "I will connect with you." She's happy to connect with people like me and get through to you, but she really wants it to be a one-to-one thing. So don't be surprised if one day you physically hear her voice in your house, because she is trying most definitely to manifest that kind of energy. You know? And it might give you a little bit of a startle when it happens because obviously we're human, but it wouldn't be anything that you would be afraid of.

I think I've probably said this twice in my lifetime as a medium … to say to someone there will come a day when you won't need me or a medium like me. This energy is so strong that you will literally see them sitting across the table with you having a cup of coffee and having a conversation. She's still got her training bands on, you know, but I know by her energy and the fact that she has no patience for this stuff. She's like, "Come on! I need to be doing my own thing here."

She's telling me she had really thick hair. She's dark and almost had like a Spanish look to her.

She's telling me about the boob, the boobs. So was there, like, an implant?

ME: Yeah.

SANDRA: Was it, like, sore? Did it have to be redone or something?

ME: I don't think it was sore?

SANDRA: Did she want them done again?

ME: She didn't express that to me.

SANDRA: She's touching here [*puts her hand on her chest*] and saying, "I'm not sure about these. I should have gotten them done again." Did she want them smaller or bigger? I have no idea.

ME: The doctor wanted her to go bigger, and she went smaller, but she was happy with them for the most part. There were some undulations in the skin, but she never mentioned having it fixed to me.

SANDRA: Okay. I can tell she's got this tenacity about her. I can just tell that.

The other thing too is that she had a lot of masculine attributes to her. Do you know what I mean? And she would have struggled with that in her teenage years and her early twenties. Some females kind of tiptoe around things, but she kicked in doors. She had a pair of cojones.

ME: I used to tell her, "You're kind of like a dude." And she was like, "No, I'm so feminine."

SANDRA: She's also showing me the New York skyline. What's the connection with that?

ME: She was born in Trenton, New York, and lived there.

SANDRA: She's giving me the feeling she stopped her education but then went back to it. Would that make any sense?

ME: Yes. She joined the U.S. Air Force. I'm going to say army because that always bugged her [*chuckling*]. It was a private joke of ours.

SANDRA: [*Laughing*]

ME: She went into the air force, and then went back and got her PhD. She served in Desert Storm.

SANDRA: Yeah. She's very proud of herself for doing that.

ME: Yeah. She was. Very proud.

SANDRA: She said it wasn't easy. She's telling me … for some reason, she keeps pointing to January. She keeps showing me January on the calendar.

ME: That's my birthday.

SANDRA: That's your birthday. Very good. Around the time of your birthday, life starts to take off in a new direction for you, and not one that eliminates her or doesn't allow room in your life. There will always be room in her life for you. She's too strong a character for that not to happen. Let me put it to you this way. She's willing to share you romantically, but if you lock the door, lock her out, she's like, "That's not happening."

ME: Yes.

SANDRA: Is there like … a Nancy?

ME: [*very surprised*] That's my aunt.

SANDRA: That's your aunt. Okay, and what was the upset with her?

ME: Oooo, she's just so harsh. I've been horrible. I have not kept in very good contact with her.

SANDRA: Ann Marie is telling you to be cautious of her. So don't feel bad. She would have this tendency to make it all about her. Do you know what I mean? [*Laughing*] I actually very much like Ann Marie. She's feisty. You know?

ME: Yeah. I sure do.

SANDRA: And she said, "Much as I used to make things about me too." [*Laughing*] And then Ann Marie started to laugh.

ME: I never laughed so much with anyone before.

SANDRA: Well, you mean the world to her, please know that. She wants you to be happy. If she were alive and you'd split up, oh yeah! There would be hell to pay then. But she knows she's in another world now. She can't fulfill all your wants and needs, and she wants you to be happy. She knows that you will be hers again.

ME: [*softly*] Okay.

SANDRA: You're going to get a hell of a lot of signs, and the majority will be from Ann Marie, and then they'll also be from other Spirit entities around you. We absolutely have Spirit guides. They are given to us before we come to Earth. They help us with our Soul agreements … so you will have signed up for this with Ann Marie. Your Soul agreed with hers, even to the traumatic ending.

Thankfully, we are born with amnesia, because if you knew when you met her that this was going to be the ending, you might go, "You know what, I'm going to give that a miss. I don't think I'm ready for that," and you might have walked away. So your Soul recognized her, and you did what you agreed to do, and then she did what she agreed to do at the end. But you will get that opportunity to have that lifetime together. In the next lifetime, you will have that happy ending.

Our Spirit guides stay with us until we die. As well, they go through our Akashic records with us—that's our life review to see what we did and what we didn't do.

October 6, 2019

Breathing Her In

In all my readings—nine in total by three different psychics—each one conveyed to me that Ann Marie used music to communicate with me. This was so true. More than anyone would ever know. I received songs I had never heard by artists I had never known existed, with the most significant and relevant lyrics about suicide, death, the Other Side, and love.

The songs would play randomly from my iPhone music library. Songs I had never purchased but were there, nonetheless. "One More Kiss, Dear" by Vangelis was one of those songs. With my headset on, I was hand-pruning a hedge at a customer's house next door to Marcy, Ann Marie's favorite customer. How, over the course of many, many years, is it possible I never heard these songs when my iPhone was on shuffle, and now I am hearing songs of such great significance and meaning? Over the course of the year, Ann Marie sent me a lot of songs while I was working at these two properties.

Here are the lyrics to this song, which conveys so much meaning.

"One More Kiss, Dear" by Vangelis

One more kiss, dear, one more sigh
Only this, dear, is goodbye
For our love is such pain and such pleasure
That I'll treasure till I die

So, for now, dear, Au revoir, ma belle
But, I vow, dear, not farewell
For in time, we may have all love's glory
Our love story to tell

Just as every autumn leaves fall from the trees
Tumble to the ground and die
So in the springtime like sweet memories
They will return, as will I

Like the sun, dear, upon high
We'll return, dear, to the sky
And we'll banish the pain and the sorrow
Until tomorrow, goodbye

One more kiss, dear, one more sigh
Only this, dear, is goodbye
For our love is such passion, such pleasure
I will treasure until I die

Like the sun, dear, upon high
We'll return, dear, to the sky
And we'll banish the pain and the sorrow
Until tomorrow, goodbye

As I mentioned, I kept a few items of Ann Marie's. Some shirts, a few pants, sweatshirts, the baseball hat she wore every day to work.

As my sister and I were going through her items and packing them for her family, I randomly pulled out this or that, along with any little item I happened across in the house that belonged to her. I keep everything neatly folded on a shelf in what used to be her walk-in closet. For the first year or more after her passing, I would go into her closet to smell her. I would pick up her hat ever so gently, place it over my face, and take a deep breath in. It was her. It was her smell. In my mind, I would sing an old Fleetwood Mac song performed by Stevie Nicks.

At the time, and for quite a while, I could not place the song. I could hear the lyrics, but I could not remember the singer. I would repeat the lines in my head while I inhaled the scent of Ann Marie on her cap: "Every night that goes between / I feel a little less / As you slowly go away from me / This is only another test / Every night you do not come / Your softness fades away." I knew one day her smell would fade from the baseball cap, and I dreaded that day.

During my first reading with Kay Fahlstrom, three months after Ann Marie's death, Kay told me that Ann Marie was communicating with me through Fleetwood Mac. Specifically, Stevie Nicks. Fleetwood Mac is one of my all-time favorite groups. That song, I later finally discovered, was titled "Storms."

On another occasion, I was with my girls. It was early in the morning, and I was making breakfast while the kids sat on the couch and watched cartoons. I typically look out our windows a lot, as our view is unbelievably amazing and quite peaceful. The green mountains and beautiful oaks, pine trees, and scrub brush. The clouds that are always changing. The fog that rests in the undulations of the hills. The birds flying by, headed to the coast over the mountains in front of them. It really is indescribable.

This particular morning, I walked to the sliding glass door, looked outside, and said, "Girls, come look! The sun is rising! Isn't it beautiful?" I try as a mother to instill in my girls the appreciation and beauty of nature. What a gift it is. As the three of us stood there looking at the sunrise, I started singing "Here Comes the Sun" by The Beatles to them.

This is highly unusual for me, as I cannot hold a tune to save my life and only sing out loud when I am alone. I'm okay with my terrible voice … or maybe I just have the volume up so high I can't hear myself.

I told the girls that this was one of my favorite songs and it was written and sung by a group named The Beatles. They thought it was a funny name. We all laughed.

Thinking nothing of it, I got the girls off to school. At the time, they were in first grade. I rushed home to take a shower and get ready for a long drive, as I had my first reading with Kay, which was on June 17, 2019. I had to get ready, drive there, have my reading, and drive back in time to pick up the kids from school.

In that reading, Kay said, "Ann Marie is sending you songs. Specifically, the song 'Here Comes the Sun' by The Beatles." Of course, my jaw dropped, and I told her not only was it one of my favorite songs, but I had just sung a portion of it to my girls that morning. Kay and I both got chills.

On another occasion, the song "Morning Fog" by Kate Bush came through. Again, I had never heard it until that day, October 20, 2019. In my journal a few days prior, I had written how I felt, almost closer to Ann Marie in a strange way. Our communication was strong and constant. It was a continual stream of our love and energy moving back and forth.

It sounds odd, but in the first year of her passing, she would put little flying bugs in my path. This happened several times while I was writing in my journal. It made me laugh, and I am sure she got a huge kick out of annoying me with little gnats and tiny flies going up my nose, landing on the rim of my glasses, and generally just being a nuisance.

One time while journaling at my kitchen table, where I always set up my journaling station, a very small fly appeared from out of nowhere and landed on the center of the rim of my reading glasses, right smack between my eyes. I sat there for a moment just chuckling to myself.

In this song, she is communicating to me not that she loves me more from the Other Side, but that she is, in an odd way, loving me better.

October 25, 2019

3358 & March 27

Ann Marie and I owned a condominium together, which was very special to us both because we had a beautiful life there. Its setting is peaceful and serene, quiet, and lovely, reminding us of Lake Tahoe. A place where the children and I have so many amazing, beautiful memories with Ann Marie. I will leave the city and the name of the street undisclosed for privacy reasons, but I will mention the house number: 3358.

Over the months, after Ann Marie's passing, when time allowed, I would look through photos of her and our family on my computer. I started branching out from my fear of computers; I'm afraid to fiddle much with anything for fear I will inadvertently delete it.

One day, when I had 30 minutes alone in my office, I came across the very first photo Ann Marie had texted me. I don't know why it took me so long to notice that the image number on the photo, IMG_3358, was the same as our condo number.

IMG_3358

The significance of our condominium and how much it meant to us both, combined with the first photo I ever received from her sharing a number is really quite unbelievable. I certainly had no idea how to change the name of an image, so this must have been assigned by the computer when I saved it.

On another occasion, again having a little free time in my office, I began looking at photos of our happy times as a family. Curious about the time and date of the second photo Ann Marie texted me when we first met, I started researching. I love this photo of her, which was the only one she used for social media accounts. I knew a little of the background, for example, that it was taken in Southern California at a special event. And I knew of one of the two gentlemen standing on either side of her, but only because I had seen him on TV. But Ann Marie had cropped them both out of the photo and enlarged it to show only her face.

Photo Date: March 27, 2015

I had learned how to get details from a photo by hovering my mouse over three small dots in the upper-right-hand corner of the photo. Doing so prompted a drop-down with a list of miscellaneous functions. One such option was "File Information." I clicked on it, hoping to learn where it had been taken. What came up was: Date Taken: March 27, 2015 … the exact day and month of her death!

This goes beyond coincidence or happenstance but could possibly be foreshadowing of future events. Ann Marie's death may have been written in her chart as one possible exit point. Maybe all this pain was written in our charts so that our Souls would grow and expand, as Kay Fahlstrom and Sandra O'Hara had mentioned.

November 9, 2019

Music Was My Best Friend

At this point, most of the music I listened to was instrumental. Music was my best friend and kept me company through my grieving.

What seemed to be the most soothing was classical piano. Brian Crain, Jon Batiste, Robin Spielberg, Fiona Joy Hawkins, Philip Wesley, David Tolk, and David Lanz are some of my favorites, though I didn't limit myself to just these pianists.

When I was alone, I played this type of music from the moment I woke in the morning until just before bed.

I don't remember why I purchased Taylor Swift's relatively new album *Lover*. Maybe I heard a song on TV and thought it sounded pretty. I have always loved her music but hadn't bought anything of hers in a few years. I was playing a little of it here and there.

On this day, I was upstairs doing laundry and remember very specifically that I had the kids, because I began to cry hysterically and thought, *I can't let the girls see me so broken down and sobbing.*

While I was sitting on the floor with my portable speaker playing music in the girls' room folding laundry, this song came on, and all the lights upstairs started flickering. The girls' overhead light, the hallway light, and the laundry room light were off-the-charts flickering.

FAITH, HOPE & LOVE

Here are the lyrics to Taylor's song "Afterglow."

"Afterglow" by Taylor Swift

I blew things out of proportion, now you're blue
Put you in jail for something you didn't do
I pinned your hands behind your back, oh
Thought I had reason to attack, but no

Fighting with a true love is boxing with no gloves
Chemistry 'til it blows up, 'til there's no us
Why'd I have to break what I love so much?
It's on your face, and I'm to blame, I need to say

Hey
It's all me in my head
I'm the one who burned us down
But it's not what I meant
Sorry that I hurt you
I don't wanna do, I don't wanna do this to you
I don't want to lose, I don't wanna lose this with you
I need to say, hey
It's all me, just don't go
Meet me in the afterglow

It's so excruciating to see you low
Just want to lift you up and not let you go
This ultraviolet morning light below
Tells me this love is worth the fight, oh

I lived like an island, punished you with silence
Went off like sirens, just crying
Why'd I have to break what I love so much?
It's on your face, don't walk away, I need to say

Hey
It's all me in my head

I'm the one who burned us down
But it's not what I meant
I'm sorry that I hurt you
I don't wanna do, I don't wanna do this to you
I don't wanna lose, I don't wanna lose this with you
I need to say, hey
It's all me, just don't go
Meet me in the afterglow

Tell me that you're still mine
Tell me that we'll be just fine
Even when I lose my mind
I need to say
Tell me that it's not my fault
Tell me that I'm all you want
Even when I break your heart

I need to say, hey
It's all me in my head
I'm the one who burned us down
But it's not what I meant
Sorry that I hurt you
I don't wanna do, I don't wanna do this to you
I don't wanna lose, I don't wanna lose this with you
I need to say, hey
It's all me, just don't go
Meet me in the afterglow

December 15, 2019

Third Reading With Jeanne Leto, Via Phone

JEANNE: I definitely have Spirit energy around me, and I know that I have your partner around me. And it's just a crazy bunch of emotions.

I'll be honest with you, I had to get rid of her last time because she was setting off things and was having a real fit, and I had to send her away. I feel her energy is different now, but … I'm not feeling her super happy, to be honest with you.

ME: Okay.

JEANNE: There's a sense of peace to a degree, but I don't know what she is disappointed about. But I feel like she is making me feel the gamut of who she was. One minute she could be great—almost like bipolar energy—and the next minute just angry and down. She's come to the Earth, like, physically. So I'm getting who she is.

I don't mean to be mean, but she wasn't the nicest person sometimes. She was very damaged. She was very hurt. I don't know if there was abuse. Physical abuse toward her at some point in her life. Or there was an alcoholic or whatever. She's kind of making me feel she was a product of what happened to her. But she excelled in other parts of her life. Here we go again … bipolar energy from being a victim to "I'm gonna show everybody I'm worth something." Does that make any sense to you?

ME: Oh yes. It's been an upsetting morning for me because I got some information with regard to people prior to her meeting me. She used to live down south, and she moved up north to be with me and the girls, and they are blaming me. They think that I participated.

JEANNE: This is why she is upset. Why I said I don't feel her so happy.

ME: Yeah. And it's really hurtful. They all think that I physically helped Ann Marie.

JEANNE: Okay. Well, this would explain why I'm not very happy and why I'm upset and kind of all over the place, and it would also make sense why I'm hearing bullshit. I did immediately feel very negative, like I said, when we started, and it would make a lot of sense because you're being cloaked with negativity, and I hope that you can kind of shake it off. I don't know where she is taking me. Maybe that you need to go see your parents and feel better.

ME: Yes.

JEANNE: She's talking about the children. She's making me feel like one might have been a little closer to her. More comfortable.

ME: Yes.

JEANNE: She is making me feel that. And she is saying she is very proud. One is more affected by everything. One is more sensitive to everything. And one is … I feel like I'm gonna dance and I love music. Like, one is overtly talented, but the other one has deep talent, because with one of them I want to draw.

ME: Yeah. Yeah. Oh yes.

JEANNE: Like, one of them you have to treat like your flowers and your plants ...

ME: Okay.

JEANNE: ... and you've gotta protect. Okay. And one of them is just more like, "I'm gonna punch you in the face—let's dance and hang out." And Ann Marie is laughing about it.

ME: Okay. Yeah. [*Chuckling*]

JEANNE: Ann Marie is laughing about it. Your daughter is like, "Give me a pony NOW, bitches!" Ann Marie is laughing. Do you understand what she's saying? "I want a unicorn now, please ... thank you."

ME: [*Laughing*]

JEANNE: Like, she's making me laugh. Do you understand what she's making me feel about the one kid?

ME: Yeah. Yeah. And she's been coming up a lot. The girls have been talking about Ann Marie a lot, and they have been telling me that they miss her. We talk about her a lot. We hung up her ornaments on the Christmas tree.

JEANNE: This is why she is bringing up the children. She is saying, "I am around those children, but there is one who lets me in more." She's backed off the one that's so sensitive because of the vibrations. The one that's so sensitive might have a little bit of panic or anxiety. So she is telling me she backs off because one of them has anxiety issues.

ME: Yeah. Nisa.

JEANNE: She's telling me that she's backed off that child because that child has anxiety, is what I just heard. And that she said, "It's not me." So you need to understand that.

ME: Yes. Okay.

JEANNE: She will not do that to that child because that child is way too sensitive and gets scared and freaked out and might have some bad dreams. Like she's saying, "No, I back off this child." You need to understand that. Nisa's feelings could get hurt easily. She feels things that aren't true because she is so sensitive. I feel like Nisa could easily cry and melt down.

ME: Mmm …

JEANNE: Ann Marie is going, "I'll watch over her. I'll take care of her." Ann Marie is saying, "This child is so sensitive, honey. She's so sensitive." The other one I feel is like a hot mess express. "She won't listen to me anyway." Like, you know, kind of laughing about it, like "Hey, if I manifested physically, she would probably hit me with a ball and laugh and say, 'Hey, you wanna play?'" Like, she's really making me have these feelings. And now I'm getting a bit of a chuckle out of her because I feel like the light comes with the children. Because I do feel like the children did ground her on some level.

She's showing me a shovel. This woman had to have actually gotten down and dirty and shoveled shit for you [*laughing*].

ME: She did—she was such a hard worker. She was a really hard worker.

JEANNE: She's making me feel like you are getting things turned around for yourself.

ME: For myself?

JEANNE: Yes. She's saying, "She's better off financially without my bullshit."

ME: [*softly*] Yeah. Yeah, 'cause I was …

JEANNE: She's saying, "I was a stress on her."

ME: … 'cause I was trying to employ her, and it caused me to get into debt. But I didn't tell Ann Marie, because I didn't want her to feel bad.

JEANNE: She knows it. And you're turning it around. She's making me feel you are turning it around and she sees it.

ME: I am.

JEANNE: And she's saying by 2020, your business is really going to do better. Like, you really are going to do better.

ME: So in our last reading, you had mentioned the names James and David. My new business partner's name is actually James David. I opened a second company since the last time we spoke.

JEANNE: See, she's saying things are getting better—there you go. Go ahead.

ME: And we just signed a contract last Thursday for a $520,000 landscape installation job.

JEANNE: Hello! Because she said by March it will get better. And it is … and she is smiling at me.

ME: Yeah. It's supposed to finish up in about three months.

JEANNE: Well, there you go. She's smiling. And I don't know why she is driving me up to Big Sur or to Carmel. But I feel like I wanna go to Carmel. I don't know why, but I'm seeing going to Carmel.

ME: We took a trip there. We didn't take a lot of trips, but that was one. We picked out our commitment rings from a little store there.

JEANNE: Okay, well she's showing it to me. So what I can tell you that happens is I get her thoughts. I get her feelings. I hear names. And she's making me smell aromas too. I don't understand why she is doing that but … this is just freakin' hilarious … why am I all of a sudden smelling, like, onions and garlic? For whatever reason.

ME: Oh. Well, I used to cook for her a lot. I remember one time I was cooking onions and garlic, just a few weeks before her passing, and she walked in the house and said, "Oh my gosh, it smells sooo good in here."

JEANNE: Okay. Well, I just feel like onions and garlic is what she made me smell. NOTHING ELSE! And she is laughing. She's like, "This is fun. You're good at this." She's showing me that you are healing. She realizes you can love somebody, but sometimes to love somebody the best thing is to move out of the way. Because she is telling me that she did cause you a lot of grief. Like, she was ruining your life.

ME: Yeah. [*softly*] We had some hard times. But I mean, I just loved her.

JEANNE: She loved you too. She realizes this is good you're moving on. And I don't know why she's showing me a lot of purple. Like, all of a sudden, I'm seeing purple. So I don't know if any of the girls like purple. She's putting all kinds of purple around me. Purple flowers. Purple. Purple. Purple. She's just cascading me with the color purple.

ME: We did … She and I painted the girls' bedroom purple, and it is also my favorite color.

JEANNE: She's smiling. She's making me feel like she'll cover the girls and protect them. But she's telling me that you are making better choices. And she's glad about that. You would make skewed choices for her. She admits it.

I don't know what is different with your hair, but she is acknowledging something about your hair.

ME: I lightened it A LOT [*laughs*].

JEANNE: She's acknowledging it.

ME: Okay. [*in a joking tone*] Does she like it?

JEANNE: She's winking at me to wink at you. And you can't see me winking [over the phone], but wink, wink, wink.

ME: Okay.

JEANNE: Yeah! She likes everything about you. She was fussy as hell about food. She was fussy! She worked for that body. Even though nobody knew she did. She worked for that body, is what I just heard.

ME: Anytime I eat something that … Like last night I was going to have ketchup, and Ann Marie's voice came into my head and said, "No, that's loaded with sugar."

JEANNE: She's laughing. "I was a freak about food." She's laughing that you would always think that your own ass was big, and she said, "I was a pain in the ass." She is telling me she was on you, and you were just really sweet. And that you know there's a lot of love here. You showed her what a good person can be.

ME: Oh … [*softly*] I tried. I really tried. Is she feeling more grounded?

JEANNE: She's feeling "freer." That's the word I heard.

December 20, 2019

The Driveway Song

You may be asking how I know when a song is sent to me by Ann Marie. There are typically a few indications. I do believe that with the universe, Jesus, or whatever name you give your higher power, communication with the Other Side is telepathic. So typically, a song will come on when I am thinking specifically of Ann Marie. Location is important as well. It could be a place where we were alone together or a place we worked together. An action like pruning roses, which we typically did side by side in the gardens. Ann Marie would always say, "Leave the roses for me!!"

With regard to the next song I'm going to mention, it took me a long time to put two and two together. I knew it was coming from Ann Marie, but I never understood why it would always play when I was in the driveway washing my truck or cleaning out the mouse cage. It took me a year to figure out the meaning behind "the driveway."

The driveway was the last place I was with Ann Marie. The medical examiner took her gently out the side gate on a gurney. It took me quite by surprise. I have no idea why, but I just assumed she would be taken out the front door. I was kept outside in the garage until the three investigators had completed their investigation. I wasn't even allowed to sit in the living room. I was not allowed inside the house at all.

It was a bitterly cold March day, and I was sitting on the cold, hard concrete floor with a sheriff's officer looking down on me while he stood. Neither of us spoke. About three hours after the police arrived on scene, while still sitting on the garage floor, I heard some commotion in the side yard by the garage and saw the side door pop open. I got up and walked over to the open gate. I just remember seeing a white bag covering Ann Marie where she lay on a gurney. My mind's eye saw her underneath it. I was in disbelief. That's the only feeling I can point to.

Even now, I have days when I ask myself, "Did that really happen? How could she have done that?"

As the examiner rolled the gurney past me, I grabbed it and wouldn't let go. The coroner's assistant didn't say anything; he simply touched my hand, and I released my grip. I watched them load her carefully into their van.

It's strange. I don't remember the details as a normal memory. I remember them as if I am watching from above or from the side. As if I weren't in my body; I was simply observing.

These are the lyrics to the song that plays frequently while I'm in my driveway.

"All We Are" by Matt Nathanson

> I tasted, tasted love so sweet
> And all of it was lost on me
> Bought and sold like property
> Sugar on my tongue

I kept falling over
I kept looking backward
I went broke believing
That the simple should be hard

All we are we are
All we are we are
And every day is the start of something beautiful

I wasted, wasted love for you
Traded out for something new
Well, it's hard to change the way you lose
If you think you've never won

All we are we are
All we are we are
And every day is the start of something beautiful

And in the end the words won't matter—no
'Cause in the end, nothin' stays the same
And in the end, dreams just scatter and fall like rain

All we are we are
All we are we are
And every day is the start of something beautiful, something real

All we are we are
All we are we are
And every day is the start of something beautiful, beautiful

Ann Marie gave life her best. I believe that with all my heart. I wish I could have imparted on her the growth my Soul has experienced in the last two to three years. But I cannot. There is no going back. These types of movements in our Souls can't be taught or explained or forced onto another. They must be experienced in order for someone to understand this type of sudden and massive growth of the Soul and expansion of consciousness.

December 24, 2019

Ann Marie's Ornaments

Christmas Eve. Our first Christmas without Ann Marie. The girls' birthday is also on Christmas, so this was a particularly hard time for me. My folks had come for a few days for support and to spend the holiday together. My mom was wonderful and so supportive. I was anticipating going through my family Christmas ornaments, which I had not seen since Ann Marie's passing. Every Christmas, she would take the children downtown to hand-paint ceramic ornaments as a Christmas gift for me. She even did a few herself.

Opening the tissue paper I had so carefully wrapped the ornaments in to keep them safe the Christmas prior was very emotional for me. I stared at the ornaments Ann Marie had painted, signed, and dated. I looked at the paint strokes and thought, *Her hand painted this … her hand once held this. She wrote these letters on the bottom.* I handled these ornaments like golden eggs. As far as I knew, no one noticed my special attention and care while hanging them on the tree.

Later that day, while my mother and I were putzing around in the kitchen, I received a text message. It was from a long-ago acquaintance of Ann Marie's who I had spoken with a time or two after her death. This is what she wrote: "Wow, I saw Ann Marie's toxicology report, and she didn't have any drugs or alcohol in her system. She must have been really unhappy with you to have done what she did."

My heart sank. I was beside myself with anger, and I fumed with hatred at this woman who had written such awful words. On Christmas Eve, no less. In fact, there was no toxicology report ever done nor was there an autopsy. I know this for certain. And if there had been, the family was much too private to share it with anyone, let alone an old acquaintance of Ann Marie's. Clearly, this must have been another rumor floating around in certain crowds.

In the past, I had always taken the high road and not given this group of women from Southern California the satisfaction of a response. Just then, while I showed my mother the text message, the dining room chandelier that we were standing under started flickering, over and over. After my mom read the text, she told me to text this woman back and tell her to go fly a kite. (Well, she didn't say it that nicely.) I was shocked that my mom told me to respond in that manner; it was so out of character for her. However, about 10 minutes later, she retracted her comment saying, "Better not to respond. Don't give them the satisfaction."

All the while, I was noticing this light flickering during our conversation while setting the Christmas dinner table.

Finally, my mom noticed too. "What's going on with this light?"

I didn't answer, but I knew it was Ann Marie telling me, "It's okay, Jenn. Don't listen to them."

My dad, meanwhile, sitting on the couch watching football, chimed in about five minutes later: "What's going on with this light in here? Must need the bulb changed." A completely different light in the living room. Needless to say, that bulb never flickered again, and though it was never changed since that day in December, it is still working fine.

I didn't say anything to anyone, but I knew. Ann Marie was with me. "Pay no mind," she would say.

In the end, I did take the high road and simply replied to the woman, "Ann Marie didn't have a toxicology report, idiot. Don't ever text me again!" I felt that was pretty mild, under the circumstances.

I thought about that text message for a long time after that day. I decided that in the end, it was better to forgive than to be weighed down by anger or hatred.

January 1, 2020

The Significance Of Numbers

By this point, 10 months had passed since Ann Marie's death. It felt like yesterday and an eternity, simultaneously. All the amazing signs around me kept me going, knowing that she was still there in Spirit. The flickering lights in the house. The dragonflies that would stop in my path, hover at eye level, and simply look at me. The birds that seemed to want to collide with my head. I can't tell you how many times I ducked because I thought I would have a beak stuck in my forehead.

In fact, it happened one time in front of a client, and I said, "Did you see that? That bird almost hit me in the head."

"Yeah, I did see that. That was odd!"

At least I was never pooped on, like Jeanne Leto joked about. I was grateful for that. The touches during the night and day. One night, I felt her entire body spooning mine. I felt touches or kisses on my eyelids and cheeks. On one occasion, the pressure on my face by my upper cheek forced the flesh on my cheekbone to push up toward my eye. I was fully awake with my eyes open. And one night, she pinched my bottom and startled me from my sleep. I am sure she got a good laugh out of that one. Another night, she pinched my nose, which woke me from a sound sleep.

Then, in late December and through the month of January, another phenomenon began to occur. I started seeing numbers. For example: 11:11, 2:22, 4:44, or 5:55. I mean, it's really hard to miss, especially when it happens several times throughout the day and night. In my journal entries from January 1 through January 5, 2020, I noted what I found on the internet about these numbers.

January 1, 2020: Journal Entry

Hello, my love. Boy, I miss you so much, my sexy woman. I felt you around today but not a lot. The big thing happening lately is the numbers I keep seeing. I either pick up my phone to make a call or wake up in the middle of the night. It seems to be happening three to five times a day.

Most consistently, I see the numbers 11:11, 1:11, 2:22, 4:44, and 5:55. So many—they're everywhere. I sit down at my computer, and it's 11:11 a.m. When I awaken in the night, it's at 1:11, 2:22, and 5:55—all in a single night.

So I am doing some research on these numbers, which I will write down on the following pages. I read that seeing three-digit number patterns is a sign you are receiving divine messages from higher realms. These angel messages are very important to you at this time of your life, and they serve as clues or guideposts to help you along your journey.

January 2, 2020: Journal Entry
Meaning Behind 1111

The number 11 is associated with faith and psychics. So 11:11 is a reminder that you are One. One with all of life and with ALL that IS.

Seeing 11:11 is an awakening call and an invitation to open your heart, raise your vibration, and tune in to this higher vibrational experience of Oneness.

Angelic beings are close by, and they want to bring you clarity and guidance. The number code for deceased loved ones to connect with you visually is 11:11. It represents columns of gates; it is a direct channel that opens between you and your Higher Self.

On the Soul level, your consciousness evolves, and you start to see life with new eyes. Instead of making decisions with your head, you start making decisions with your heart. For this reason, you begin to see the illusion of life and the true divine reality of all that is. You are moving to a higher energetic vibration. The universe is listening to your thoughts. Thinking is the manipulation of energy; hence, a thought is a willful act, and it is powerful enough for creation.

January 3, 2020: Journal Entry
Meaning Behind 222

The meaning of number 222 suggests that you are at a point in your life where you are looking for some balance. This means it is the best time to have faith and to keep trusting. 222 is commonly related to the beginning of expansion that reflects growth in a certain area of your life. It is a divine sign letting you know that a new cycle is about to begin. This new cycle of experiences is about growth and expansion. The seeds of your thoughts are growing.

It is important to realize that your thoughts become your words, and through your words, you express the creative power within you to manifest everything around you. On this path of 222, you are being reminded to take steps toward loving yourself, accepting yourself, and forgiving yourself.

In the whole scheme of things, all your relationships begin with your primary connection to the Divine Source. It is the core relationship that establishes your purpose for existing in this life.

January 4, 2020: Journal Entry
Meaning Behind 444

You are on the right path of spiritual awakening. You have become more aware of the Spirit within you, and you are feeling the subtle energies of the universe. The number 444 is here to tell you that you are awakening, and you are on the right track of entering another dimension on a higher spiritual plane. That your guardian angels are close by. You are resonating with the universe in perfect synchronicity. You are living a truly harmonic moment with creation, and you are ready to unravel its deepest mysteries. You have become aware of the spiritual dimension and the energies within and around you. Most important, this means you've reached the point in your life where you are ready to transcend personal limitations. Three-digit numbers also commonly show up after the death of a loved one.

January 5, 2020: Journal Entry
Meaning Behind 555

Things in your life will start to make a shift and change to make room for new and better things coming to you. Keep in mind that your new path will be revealed to you one step at a time. You are in the process of significant change, and new events will be shown to you at divine timing. Seeing 555 is an angelic reminder that you are a divine, infinite being who chose to incarnate here on Earth to experience life in human form.

Always feel you have worth because you are here to cocreate with the Universal Source and complete a life mission. 555 is the number of Jesus Christ. The name Jesus Christ adds up and breaks down to 5. Jesus has 5 letters. Jesus gracefully took 5 loaves of bread to feed 5,000 people, and later, at the end of his life, He had 5 wounds on the cross. Thus, 555 represents grace and redemption; 555 also means to be prepared. A major shift is about to come into your life experience and change your path's direction.

So seeing 555 means that it is not what happens to you that defines you, but what you make of it. No matter what life throws at you, the most important thing is your state of being. The truth is that your state of being creates your circumstances, and not the other way around.

March 24, 2020

A Double Rainbow

After Ann Marie passed, there were several people I was desperate to reach but had no way of doing so. Ann Marie's phone was with her family, and I had never contacted these people directly. One such person was Shira.

I had met Shira a few months prior to Ann Marie's death, when Ann Marie and I drove down south to see some of her old friends. Shira is a lovely, wise, and kind woman who was somewhat of a guru, therapist, and mentor to Ann Marie. Ann Marie trusted and admired her greatly. Shira's profession is psychotherapy, which she now offers for free, as she desires and is able to give back to the community.

Ann Marie was director of nursing and clinical services for Lindora Clinics in Southern California. She had a Doctor of Philosophy degree and was a family nurse practitioner. She was very proud of those degrees and worked hard to achieve those goals. Shira was one of her patients. By Ann Marie's account, the two of them connected as if they had been best buddies their entire lives. Shira was psychically inclined and said that the two had known each other in a past life as American Indians.

I had reached out to Julie, a private detective I had used in the past, to help me find Shira. Having not heard back from Julie, I decided to try an online company, PeopleFinders. I entered all the information I knew about Shira and had no luck. Nothing.

One day while cleaning up emails, I came across the folder titled "Ann Marie." I was thrilled and immediately began perusing our email exchanges. To my great surprise and relief, I came across an email Ann Marie had forwarded to me from Shira. It was of amazing insects and animals that took on the form of other things, like a praying mantis that looked like an angel. Now I was able to email Shira, which I did straightaway. Sadly, the email was returned; it was an inactive email address.

I was heartbroken. I wondered if maybe she had passed away, as she was in her late eighties. In rereading the email, I noticed a phone number, which I assumed belonged to one of Shira's friends. So I called the number. A woman answered, and I explained that I was desperate to communicate with Shira but had no way of contacting her. I told the woman that Shira and I had a mutual friend who had passed away. I gave her my number and asked that she please pass it along to Shira.

A few months went by with no word. I had exhausted all avenues without success for almost a year. On March 24, I decided to try Shira's email again. (Clearly, I am not one to give up easily.) I also sent a prayer out to the universe for a little help. It was three days from the one-year anniversary of Ann Marie's death, and I was yearning to speak with someone close to her.

Within an hour of sending my second email, I received a response from Shira: "Good to hear from you. Please feel free to call me."

I was nervous and thought, *You found her. Now, how are you going to tell her?* I drove home, palms sweating and heart pounding. I situated myself on the edge of our couch next to the living room sliding glass door, where I had the best reception. With shaking fingers and a lump in my throat, I dialed the number.

As soon as Shira answered, she asked, "Is Ann Marie okay?"

Just then the most amazing, vivid rainbow appeared right off my back deck. It looked close enough to touch.

I replied, "She passed away, and she knows we are talking right now. I am looking at the brightest, most beautiful rainbow I have ever seen."

Minutes later, a second rainbow shone above it. A double rainbow. As I watched, they became brighter and brighter. The thought of my and Ann Marie's song, "Double Rainbow" by Katie Perry, came to mind, and I cried tears of joy.

After speaking with Shira a few minutes, I told her I had to hang up so I could capture these rainbows. I was able to get videos and photos of them. When I was done, I called her back. I told her how I had been trying to reach her for so long without success.

We spoke for about 15 minutes. As soon as I hung up that second time, the double rainbows disappeared. God, Jesus, the universe, and Ann Marie connected Shira and me, and I was so grateful to have the opportunity to speak to someone who had been such an important part of her life.

April 14, 2020

Fourth Reading With Jeanne Leto, Via Phone

JEANNE: This morning when I got up at 4 a.m., I actually saw her. Normally I don't see … I've seen spirits, and they are not in color, and they are transparent, but I literally saw your girlfriend, your partner. She's shorter than me and very slim. She's a pretty woman. She has shoulder-length dark hair and she's just really, really pretty. She's got good arms. I'll die asking someone to pluck my chin and do my hair and please tuck my arms [*laughing*]. I'm serious—tuck my arms [*more laughing*].

ME: [*Laughing*]

JEANNE: She was following me around. She was beautiful. She had dark hair. It was like brunette, but darker when she was younger. She really likes me a lot, and I was laughing because she's following me around. I'm getting coffee and I literally saw her coming down my hallway, and she kind of followed me around, and I said, "We're good." She's about 5'7" I would think. When I had to use the restroom, she backed off because I was like, "Excuse me." I felt her heightened energy. But for her to physically manifest in an image takes a lot of fuckin' energy. This girl was very determined.

ME: She was a strong woman.

JEANNE: Fuck, yeah … very determined. Very determined.

ME: That was one of her really positive qualities. I loved that about her.

JEANNE: She's got high hopes ... like, there goes another rubber [tree] plant. She's very determined.

ME: About a week ago, I swear I felt her. I woke up in the middle of the night because I felt this pressure against my back, my bottom, and my legs. I was lying on my side. And I swear, I kind of hopped up because I was shocked—it felt like she was spooning me.

JEANNE: I just heard the word "snuggling." (I'm gonna call her Annie.) She put a big white lily in front of me. She's also putting the number 20 in front of me as being significant to her.

ME: That's her birthday: May 20.

JEANNE: Okay. She's saying, "I'm really feeling like I'm like an Earth angel." I'm getting so cold. I feel that she is very active because she does love you very much. She is in a very good space. She did go away for a while because she had to do a lot of work, but she was around. And I'm laughing because she's saying, "Sorry I scared that one woman off, but I didn't like her."

ME: I know. I know. And I did feel her go away, but I've felt her a lot the last two weeks. And Roni was so scared, she never stayed the night again. So I had to face any fears I had and stay here alone when I didn't have the kids.

JEANNE: Well, she's back. She's saying, "This is my time. Your time. I did my work. I am very happy. I'm very much at peace." She's saying, "I am with the Lord. I am with God. I am with Jesus. I am. I am." She's saying, "I am." She must have been raised Catholic, because when I said Mother Mary—when I prayed earlier—she had a connection to

Mother Mary. Someone in her family was close to Mother Mary. Her family prayed to Mary. But she's … I almost have to say, she's being a little cocky. "Cocky" is the word she's saying and she's laughing about it. What does the name Rose mean?

ME: Um, well, I'm talking to a woman whose name is Rosa.

JEANNE: There we go, because she's saying Rose. Rose. She's being funny. I feel like she kind of … I hate to say what she's making me feel. She's kind of trying to manipulate your love life. Not in a bad way, but she's kind of trying to pick out your partner for you. I hate to tell you, because she's making me feel like you're picking some dunces.

ME: [*Laughing*] Okayyy. Oh shit.

JEANNE: She's not super excited about anyone in your life, is what I'm hearing. She's saying you can do better than that. And she's telling me you can go a little younger this time. She thinks it would be good for you. She's saying you need someone who can be there for you, and for the girls as well. To have energy for the children. I'll have to use the cards to interpret what she means because there is a veil and it's just like BAM! BAM! BAM! Just like I heard the name Rose, I'm hearing all these names. I don't know what "Martha" is or … Marg? Like, she's throwing names at me. Juan. You know, it's like SNAP, SNAP, SNAP.

ME: Marg is her twin sister, and Martha is her mother. Juan is her father.

JEANNE: And she's saying, "Anyone that knows you and knows me knows that I was crazy." Annie is telling me she was a little crazy. Everybody knew it. She was a little bipolar, and she was a terrible drunk. And she says, "I can admit it now. I can admit it now."

ME: Yes. Yeah.

JEANNE: This is so weird. Why is she showing me a cow? I just saw a rainbow, and now she's showing me a Guernsey cow? I don't understand.

ME: Ah … Nisa has a Guernsey cow stuffed animal that she sleeps with every night. And when I make the girls' bed in the morning, I put the Guernsey cow on the bed next to a stuffy rabbit that Ann Marie bought Ella. And after Ann Marie died, Ella made a little shirt for it that reads "LOVE." Nisa sleeps with her cow, and Ella sleeps with the bunny rabbit from Ann Marie.

JEANNE: There you go. I heard "Yes." She says, "Touché. Good job." 'Cause I'm like, she's showing me a cow. Why is she showing me a cow? 'Cause she loves the children, and you know, she is acknowledging them. She is going to be there for their half-yearly birthday. She says, "Of course, Mom. Of course, Mom." She's telling me, "Watch the balloons because it hurts the environment." For whatever reason, she's very much into the environment now and protecting it.

ME: She was before, when she was alive.

JEANNE: She's saying, "Balloons kill birds. Don't let them have balloons."

ME: Okay. Okay. I won't do that. Even this morning when I flushed the toilet, I was like, ah—Ann Marie would tell me not to flush it.

JEANNE: She gets an actual kick out of me having all these animals and stuff. You know cleaning and stuff. So she definitely is into animals. One hundred percent.

ME: Oh yeah, for sure.

JEANNE: I'm hearing it was a part of her life. They were what made her have peace. They helped her.

ME: Yeah.

JEANNE: She is showing me birds. So I don't know if you have bird feeders and stuff, but she's showing me little birds and feeders and she is acknowledging these things.

ME: I do. I do. You know, when she first passed away, I had many, many birds come straight for my head. Like, I literally had to duck because I thought I was going to get hit in the face. I tell you, my whole life that has never happened to me, and then all of a sudden, it's happening all the time. And I do have tons of bird feeders. Watching the birds at the feeders is so peaceful for me.

JEANNE: It's her, it's her!

ME: I know. It even happened at a client's house. I said to him, "Did you see that?" And he said, "Yeah!"

JEANNE: She's laughing. She says, "None of them have hit yet. They haven't." She says, "I can't promise them not shitting." She's being funny. "I can't promise one might not shit …" [*Laughing*]

ME: [*Laughing*] I know.

JEANNE: She's laughing. She's showing me white teeth. She had nice teeth. She had good teeth.

ME: I know. [*in a sad whisper*] Oh yeah, she had beautiful teeth.

JEANNE: I'm sorry. Don't get sad 'cause I feel like she's trying to be funny and cute to try to perk you up. It's terrible. She's here to help you, but it took her killing herself to find her peace, which is terrible, and it didn't happen right away over there either.

And I don't know why she's talking about clocks. I don't know if she's messing with clocks or doing something around them. Whether it's phones …

ME: She messes around with my computer a lot and my phone. Oh! I have one client who Ann Marie winter-pruned the Joseph's Coat Climbing Rose in their garden. It was a big job. The irrigation clocks keep changing, and no one knew who was doing it. I told my client she must have a ghost. I finally put a handwritten note in all three clocks saying: "Please DO NOT TOUCH THESE CLOCKS." And guess what? It stopped.

JEANNE: That was her. She's talking about just messing with stuff. To her, she's not being mean. She just wants you to know "I'm there. I'm there. I'm there."

ME: Oh no. No, I never see anything as being mean.

JEANNE: She's showing me a bunch of greens as far as food. So I don't know if she is bringing me to the kids and their diet? Incorporating greens. She's talking about greens and vegetables. She's a little stickler about some of the shit you're feeding them.

ME: Yeah. Okay. I have to get better about that with myself and the kids. I've kind of fallen off the wagon with my diet. I used to be good. Yes, I totally know what she is saying.

JEANNE: She's throwing greens and little carrots. I feel that this woman really… vegetables were very important to her. And garlic.

ME: Like, what?

JEANNE: Like using garlic and oils.

ME: Yes. We loved garlic. I used to take a whole garlic clove and cut the top off, put a little olive oil in it and bake it, and we would eat that.

JEANNE: She's making me feel it's good for your gut too. Now don't get mad, 'cause I've never seen you. She says you know you put weight on your ass and legs. Like, she's laughing. And she's saying, "Carbs are not her friend." Like, you must be a carb person when you feel bad.

ME: Oh, man! I've been eating some potato chips. When I am upset, I go for carbs not sugar.

JEANNE: She's laughing. She's saying the more the cushion for the pushin'. She's being funny about it [*laughing*]. She says she wants you to take care of those kids and eat better. And tomatoes too. She's showing me a juicy tomato. So she must have loved to cut up tomatoes and put them in olive oil. She's making me hungry, actually.

ME: [*Laughing*] I started last week. I bought a bunch of asparagus and broccoli, because I knew. I knew that I wasn't doing very well. And we've been sitting down for breakfast, lunch, and dinner at the table. You know, 'cause we are homeschooling and everything now. So everybody is home all the time.

JEANNE: I just heard, "Tell her I approve. Tell her I approve." It has nothing to do with your looks. She's saying it's your cardio health, because I feel like she's saying there are people in your family that have cardio issues. She says, "You're getting older, you need to be there for our children." She feels like she had quite some time with them and developed quite a relationship. She makes me feel you need to be healthy and strong. The girls are young, and you have a long time to go to take care of them, is what she's making me feel. So it's all about health. She's saying, "Please tell her I think she's beautiful."

ME: Okay. Okay. I just started taking her vitamin pills like two or three days ago. They were in the cupboard.

JEANNE: She says, "Horse pills" or something. I don't know what that means.

ME: Well, they're pretty big. The pills.

JEANNE: [*Laughing*] Horse pills.

ME: And I'm taking zinc and calcium.

JEANNE: She's being funny again. Like when I said, "Horse pills," she goes, "The bigger the better." She's laughing. The bigger the better.

ME: Oh my gawd!

JEANNE: Inside joke. She's still being funny. She's got a good personality. She is funny.

ME: [*Laughing*] I can't believe she said that!

JEANNE: She says, "No shame in my game." She's being really funny. She's saying, "I'm cute. I'm cute."

ME: She is cute.

JEANNE: She's singing, "You are the apple of my eye." Jesus. Gawd. She's singing Stevie Wonder all of a sudden.

ME: [*Laughing*]

JEANNE: Gawd. Jesus. [*Laughing*]

ME: Does she know that I … she had the "Jesus Calling" prayer book that she read every day. I have it and it's hers. I read it every day.

JEANNE: She's telling me, "Anything with Jesus. Go, girl. Go, girl!" I have my Bible here and she's pointing to it. She says those are the light spirits. Those are the light ones. And she's singing, "You are the apple of my eye. Forever you'll stay in my heart." I can't with her [*laughing*]. I can't. I'm like, seriously? You can't make this shit up. Like, I'm out of my mind.

ME: [*Laughing*] I could see her doing that.

JEANNE: She is. She's singing, "You are the apple of my eye," and I'm sitting here like ice cold, and she's laughing. She's laughing at us. She gets a kick out of it. She does like me, I have to say. She really does. She likes my energy.

ME: I bet she does.

JEANNE: I'm glad she likes me too, 'cause I wouldn't want to piss her off.

[*We laugh together.*]

JEANNE: Why is she showing me hostas? Why is Annie showing me hostas?

ME: The plant?

JEANNE: Yeah.

ME: I don't know. I love hostas.

JEANNE: She says, "Play the field. Have fun." She'll bring you the right one. You will be a bride again. Mark my words. She's saying don't be a bridezilla and get someone to do your flowers.

[*We are laughing hysterically.*]

JEANNE: [*Laughing*] She's a mess. She's a mess, this girl. She's hilarious. Now come on, that was a funny reading. Now stop it. She had some good one-liners.

ME: [*Laughing*] I know. Oh my gosh. She sure did.

JEANNE: I just have to take a picture of my cat, Annie, who is always hiding. Look pretty, stinky. Look pretty. She came out 'cause your woman is here. She never comes out. Never. Me and Ann Marie would have been buddies. I would adopt a frickin' llama if I could.

ME: I know. Our dream was to have an animal sanctuary. Ann Marie had it all set up, the logo and everything. It was called Caring Hearts Animal Rescue. I didn't find that out until after her passing. I was quite surprised, because I did not know she had gone to all that work to register it and everything.

April 21, 2020

Third Reading With Kay Fahlstrom, Via Phone

KAY: Ann Marie says, "Hello, babe." She's very happy to talk to you again. She really enjoys these meetings. I know you guys talk as well. I know you get a lot from her, but she's very excited to be able to use my voice, so to speak, to say what she wants to say.

ME: Yes.

KAY: Ann Marie makes me feel that visiting at night is a big thing. As you're falling asleep, you're thinking of her. In the middle of the night, you think of her. When you wake up, you're thinking of her. She's telling me all this.

ME: Yes. That is so true. I do that every night. Yup.

KAY: So that's a rich time of hanging out and visiting. Okay.

ME: Yes. Mmm.

KAY: Now um … there's something about waving. Are you waving at her sometimes? Like, do you wave with your hand? Like, "Hi, Ann Marie." Or is it like, "Hello. I know you are there." Something like either she's waving at you or you're waving at her. Do you ever do that?

ME: When I feel her presence around me, I lift my arm up in her direction and reach for her.

KAY: She's like, "I can see you. We can see each other. I can see you. I see you do that." Like, "Hi, I know you're there." And she's like, "I'm there! I'm there!" You already know that, but she wants me to reiterate that.

ME: Yeah, yeah.

KAY: She says the girls send her thoughts.

ME: Yes. They tell me they do.

KAY: Like "We miss you. We love you, and we remember you." And Ann Marie loves that. She is like, "I can hear them, and I am getting their messages."

ME: Yes. They tell me, and I tell them that is great. They ask her for things. Like to win a prize at school or something. And Ella won, like, these silly little prizes four times in one day—out of the whole class. It was unbelievable. She came home and told me, said she had asked Ann Marie for help.

KAY: Yup. Absolutely.

ME: You know, Ella will come home from school and say, "I was talking to Ann Marie today." And you know, she tells me these things. And I'm like, "Cool. I am pleased Ella is open to all this. I let them come to me, though—I don't try to influence them in any way.

KAY: Nisa is helped by Ella talking about it. Because then Nisa is like, "Oh, it's okay to talk to Ann Marie and talk about her, and it's okay to feel like she's contacted us or she's on the breeze." So Nisa is kind of getting educated by Ella.

ME: Okay. Good. Good.

KAY: Ann Marie says, "Jenn, you're a treasure to me. I love you just the same. I am so sorry my torment got in the way."

ME: [*softly*] Yeah. Oh hm …

KAY: She feels very bad about that. Almost like how the torment got added into the relationship. She's just acknowledging that. The most important thing to me as a medium is she gets to say what is healing for her, and hopefully it's healing for you. I ask her some questions. "How do you come through to Jenn?" and I say, "Hey, I'm here, I love you." I feel like you can feel her, right?

ME: Oh yeah! She went away for a while, and then she kind of came back like gangbusters.

KAY: [*Laughing*]

ME: She came back right around the one-year anniversary of her passing.

KAY: She says she also comes through to you with small animals. Like when you are out there doing your work. She's showing lizards.

ME: Oh, that's really weird 'cause I went on a hike, and there were just lizards everywhere. Baby lizards. I even filmed them. The abundance was the odd thing about it. I felt it was Ann Marie. And I was hiking yesterday, and they kept darting across my path. I almost stepped on one. I even texted a friend. She probably thinks I'm nuts! But I knew it was Ann Marie. I'm like, *This is Ann Marie*. After all this time and all the amazing things that have happened to me, I am still in awe when she sends me signs.

KAY: Yup. Well, Ann Marie is behind it. You know some people would think that the animal IS Ann Marie. I myself do not believe that.

ME: I don't think it's her; I just think it's her getting my attention.

KAY: Right! Absolutely. She's influencing the lizard to come near you. You can tell your friend that a medium asked, "Ann Marie, how do you come through to Jenn?" And the first thing she showed me was a lizard. You can use that to corroborate. Because again, out of thousands and thousands of readings, I've probably said that probably just once or twice, maybe three times tops, over all these years.

ME: Oh I will. I will tell her.

KAY: She's also showing me … she calls it "the stereo." Music. The stereo. Okay.

ME: Hm. Okay.

KAY: She says something about playing a song again and again. She gives the feeling of songs with the feeling of like "We're never apart. We're still together. Like, I'm here. You're there. But we're never apart. We're still connected." She's also saying, "Sweet wonderful you" and Fleetwood Mac.

ME: Oh yeah. Yeah.

KAY: Songs with lyrics like "We're still connected." She LOVES using music and making you hear songs and lyrics.

ME: Yeah. It happens all the time. We were at the park last week, and I had gotten the girls new bicycles, and it was a beautiful day. I was thinking of her. And the girls were just going around and around on their bicycles, and I was just thinking, *These bikes are from Ann Marie. I want to give these bikes to the girls from Ann Marie.* Then this beautiful song came on my headset. And the song title was "Her." And I knew that was Ann Marie telling me she was there at that moment with us.

In fact, I bought a painting last year at an art and wine festival, and I went to go get cash and came back, and the artist said, "You should consider this one too." It was a painting of white Iceberg roses. Ann Marie had pruned tons of Iceberg roses in the gardens. And I looked on the back of the painting and it was called "Her."

So back to being at the park with the kids going around and around. After the song ended, another really pretty song came on called "Home." The next song was called "Free." Things such as this happen to me a lot.

KAY: Oh my God. WOW! Absolutely. I don't know what she means by … Do you play certain songs over and over?

ME: Oh yeah. I'm so bad. I have such a high tolerance for repetitiveness [*laughing*]. I can listen to a song over and over. Some songs, like our song by Katy Perry, "Double Rainbow," I play over and over.

KAY: Well, it's comforting. She says, "Play it again."

ME: Okay.

KAY: There's something about a machine having lapses. I ask Ann Marie, "At work? At home? Or what?" I feel like she's saying it is at work.

ME: Ohhh … shoot. It's my work truck. José keeps telling me that sometimes it doesn't start. I've got to get it into the shop. But I just spent $2,000 getting it tuned up, and then we got it back, and now he's telling me that it's not starting. It's happened three times. Yeah. It's my work truck. I just haven't had the money or the time to take it in and have it checked. I'm trying to stretch it as long as I can.

KAY: It's a good heads-up. It's something you can take care of. But I get you on the money thing.

ME: Yeah.

KAY: She's showing me—it's kind of humorous in a way—she's showing me that you're kind of shifting around. Like trying to get comfortable. I feel like you're shifting around. And you're like, "No, that's not quite right. I need to move over here, and I need to go that way and I need to go this way." I don't know if this is at work? Or you're seated somewhere? Or if you are working in an awkward position? But she's showing me you kind of shifting around. And she's like, "Oh my God, can you get comfortable?!" I don't know what this is?

ME: Mmm … probably at work. I have a little chair. It's special because it was her chair for work. OH, YESTERDAY! I got our couples therapist, Jan, as a new client. And I often wonder if she would visit me there. I was working on a fern that was on a little hill. Both directions. So I kept shifting the chair around. And I thought, *I'll go to the other side, and I'll work uphill instead of downhill.* Then I was working uphill, but it was still uncomfortable. And I kept trying my chair in different spots, but nothing was working. I think that's what she's talking about. It was quite a scene.

KAY: Yeah. 'Cause she's showing you shifting around on a seat. She saw that whole thing. She's laughing about it. She saw that whole thing. [*Laughing*]

[*We laugh together.*]

KAY: Oh my gosh, we are running out of time. I need to speed up. She loves you off the charts. So what was it like to hear from her today?

ME: Amazing as always. Totally amazing.

KAY: You guys … you have such a great connection.

June 1, 2021

My Desktop Has A Mind Of Its Own

I have stopped journaling. I promised myself I would journal for one year from the time of Ann Marie's passing, and I kept that promise. I'm reminded of one of my favorite movies, *Forrest Gump*, when Forrest started jogging and ran for a year then just stopped out of the blue one day in the middle of nowhere. I felt like that. One day, I just woke up and the strong desire to journal was gone. So I just stopped. I continue to experience amazing and beautiful things, but I stopped writing about them. I do, however, typically make note of the occurrence with video or photos.

It was June 1, a Tuesday, and it started like any other day. I didn't have the kids, so I was up early and off to work. When I arrived home, I went straight to my office as I usually do to stay caught up with work and answer emails. If I were to sit down after a hard day of labor, it's likely that I would stay sitting, only to get up for dinner. Often when I turn my computer on and punch in my password, my desktop will have small green check marks in the lower-left-hand corner of my files.

I have about 40 Word document files on my desktop, and about 21 of Ann Marie's. Shortly after her passing, her Word files changed on their own to PDF files. I have not touched or moved any of her files since her death.

About a year ago, I asked the computer guy, who makes house calls and periodically cleans up the cookies on my computer, "What are these little green check marks on each file?" He told me the computer does it automatically as it backs up the files and sends them up to the cloud.

Okay, makes complete sense to me, I thought at the time and dismissed it from my mind.

Well, on this Tuesday at 3:38 p.m. (according to my iPhone time stamp), instead of the small green check marks in the lower-left-hand corner of all my and Ann Marie's files, it was the second photo Ann Marie had sent me when we first began dating. The one she had used for her social media profile picture. So in total, there were about 60 little photos of her all over my desktop.

I did manage to take a clear video of it, and I am so glad I had the wherewithal to do so, because I was quite taken aback and in shock. Another gift, indeed. Ann Marie was with me this day, sending her love and letting me know she was right there with me.

September 23, 2021

Darling, It's Me—One Last Song

I was home alone, working in the kitchen. I typically try not to cry in front of anyone. I mean, I rarely ever do, but sometimes it comes without warning and is beyond my control.

It has been almost two and a half years now that Ann Marie has been gone. I have a wonderful new partner who is amazing in every way and so understanding and accepting of Ann Marie. As I mentioned, I happened to be alone this day, which is a rare occasion. I started to cry very loudly, knowing no one was around to hear me. I cannot remember what triggered it—it may have been something as simple as seeing a beautiful bird outside the window that made me think of Ann Marie. Two and a half years might seem like a long time to some, but for me, it felt like I had lost her yesterday.

To this day, I really do not listen to music with lyrics; instead, I prefer soothing piano instrumentals for the most part. Ask my family—they are so sick of hearing it, but they let me play it anyway.

On this day, my partner had turned the Sonos stereo on for the puppy dogs on a station called Coffee House Radio. The station plays mellow, soothing music for the pups when we are out of the house. As I was crying in the kitchen doing the dishes or preparing dinner (I don't remember which), a song came on that really stood out to me. I could clearly hear the words "Darling, don't you cry." This term of endearment, *darling*, Ann Marie and I had used every day. I walked over to the couch and sat down so I could hear the lyrics more clearly.

This is what I heard.

"Darling" by Halsey

Really can't remember where I left my spine
Carrying my body in a bag for dimes
Hidden in the pages of *The New York Times* at home

Maybe I'll be better if I take my meds
Ain't a double header if you lose your head
Tried a medication that I bought instead
It's working for a little but there's not much left

Darling, don't you weep
There's a place for me
Somewhere we can sleep
See you in your dreams

Ever since a little girl, I found it sweet
Driving past a graveyard on a lonesome street
All the little flowers gave me something to believe in

Never knew the feeling of a stable home
Been a couple years of living on the road
Couldn't really tell you where they'd leave a stone
To visit me when I am dead and gone

Darling, don't you weep
There's a place for me
Somewhere we can sleep
See you in your dreams

Darling, don't you cry
Head fast toward the light

Foolish men have tried
But only you have shown me how to love being alive

Until it's time to see the light
I'll make my own with you each night
I'll kidnap all the stars, and I will keep them in your eyes
I'll wrap them up in velvet twine
And hang them from a fishing line
So I can see them any time I'd like

Darling, don't you weep
There's a place for me
Somewhere we can sleep
I'll see you in your dreams

Darling, don't you cry
Head fast toward the light
Foolish men have tried
But only you have shown me how to love being alive

I started crying even harder. After I calmed down, I took the words to heart.

There is a place for Ann Marie, and she is happy and at peace now on the Other Side, still watching over the girls and me. I had never heard this song before and had never heard of the artist.

I always told Ann Marie that ALL I ever wanted was her happiness, no matter what that looked like for me, since I wholeheartedly believe in a Heaven, and that is where her Soul resides. She is truly happy and at peace.

I am so grateful that Ann Marie shared this song with me.

January 16, 2022

Birthday Wishes

Ann Marie continues to communicate with me to this very day. Not as often, but still quite a bit. I still talk to her every day.

January 16, 2022, was my third birthday without her. I have a digital clock that sits below the TV on the wall in our bedroom. I never use it as an alarm clock … ever. Not even once. I typically wake up very early, so it is never required. On the off chance that I do need to use an alarm, I use my iPhone.

At exactly midnight on January 16, 2022, the digital clock alarm went off. Ann Marie was the first person to wish me a happy birthday—granted, via a static radio station that woke me from a deep sleep and scared me and my partner half to death.

Ann Marie probably found that funny. I am sure she got quite a chuckle out of it. Nonetheless, thank you, darling, for the birthday wishes.

About The Author

 **Jennifer "Jenn" France** was born in Sacramento, California, and was raised in the small town of Davis, California, home of the University of California (UC), Davis. Both of her parents worked at UC Davis in the department of pomology, a branch of botany dedicated to the study of growing fruit and nuts.

After graduating Davis Senior High School in 1988, Jenn attended a local community college before transferring to UC Davis, where she majored in psychology.

Jenn's life took a major turn when she left college to run her own business in the San Francisco Bay Area. She has successfully owned and operated Jenn's Gardening for more than 33 years. During the summer of 2002, she worked as an apprentice under master gardener and rosarian Lindi S. Reagan, and in 2003, she received her Certificate of Graduation from Unique University for installation and maintenance in low-voltage lighting. Additionally, she obtained her State of California Contractors License in May 2004, after passing both the legal and trade portions of the exams.

In 2006, facing challenges with gathering plant materials in a timely fashion for her landscape installation jobs, Jenn had a revolutionary idea that would streamline the acquisition of plant material for landscape companies. That year, Green Order Complete was born, a single source company that would supply wholesale plants and trees delivered direct to landscape job sites across the San Francisco Bay Area.

Today, Jenn continues to divide her time between running her landscaping business and raising her twin 10-year-old daughters.

Besides gardening, she has a passion for knowledge and continues to learn all she can about the afterlife and the Other Side. Jenn plans to write additional books on this subject.

Faith, Hope & Love is her first book. You can contact her through her website at JennFranceWrites.com.

Acknowledgments

To the very best of my ability, I have written this book with pure and truthful honesty, in the hopes that when my children are of the age to learn the extent of Ann Marie's passing, they will read it. And if they desire, they can listen to my recorded readings and read my diary to corroborate its accuracy.

I've always called *Faith, Hope & Love* "Ann Marie's book" because for me, it *is* her book. I have experienced something very profound that in some instances can be considered subjective, which is why I have attempted to intertwine experiences that are more objective, either through witnesses or physical photographic proof.

I would like to thank the many people who supported me through my journey, which continues to this day. The friends and family who helped in any way they were able.

My mother, Valerie Stallman, who always remained strong for my sake and always listened.

My sister and brother-in-law, Leslie and Scott Donald, who are always by my side.

To my therapist, Michele Kirk, MFT, for her support and gentle guidance. And thank you to the many leaders and organizers of suicide support groups I attended.

Thank you to the many strangers who came into my life, even if only to be an angel passing through at just the right moment in time to help with my healing process.

And thank you to the three psychic mediums who helped in my grieving process and were there almost from the start.

Thank you to my daughters, who are so patient with me and have such words of wisdom at such a young age. And lastly, thank you to Shannon Lee Kampa for coming into our lives, for her unique patience, and for always supporting me through my grief.

Medium Biographies

Jeanne Leto, Medium

Jeanne Leto is an intuitive who has been helping clients since having a near-death experience more than 15 years ago. Her clients include various law enforcement officials, private investigative groups, medical doctors, celebrities, and private citizens, in both the United States and worldwide.

Jeanne is a reader for Justice Served Private Investigations (North Carolina) and Truth-Justice Investigations (Virginia). She's been nominated as America's Best Reader several times at Edgar Cayce's Association for Research and Enlightenment. She has shot a TV pilot, developed show ideas, and taught on angels and angel card reading. She has written two books, *Angel Chills* and *Hope Angels*, which are compilations of true supernatural stories.

Jeanne wishes to empower her clients and help them get answers from God by growing their intuition.

Jeanne can be reached at JeanneLetoHopeAngels.com.

Kay Fahlstrom, Medium

Kay Fahlstrom is a psychic medium who miraculously survived a near-death experience (NDE). While intuitive before this experience, in her early twenties, Kay developed her gifts as a psychic and medium over the years following her NDE—which she chronicled in the entertaining book *Reborn A Medium* (available on Amazon). Kay pursued formal training as a medium with local teachers in the San Francisco Bay Area, and studied with world-renowned psychic mediums such as James Van Praagh, and extensively with Lisa Williams. Kay was certified as an evidential medium by Williams in the Lisa Williams International School of Spiritual Development, after many classes of escalating difficulty (over several years).

Kay offers readings to clients from all over the United States and abroad. The readings can be messages from loved ones who crossed over and/or guidance about relationships, career, or living situations (and can include both types of readings). As a professional with integrity, clarity, and passion, Kay connects with people and puts them at ease. During readings, Kay sometimes mentions a reminder of their Spirit loved one's sense of humor from an inside joke or story. Afterward, Kay often receives spontaneous feedback that clients feel a renewed sense of connection, comfort, peace, and healing.

Kay can be reached via her Facebook page.

Sandra O'Hara, Medium

Sandra O'Hara was an Irish psychic, tarot reader, and medium who had communicated with spirits since she was four years old. For more than 30 years, she was a well-known, well-respected psychic both in the UK and in America.

Sandra was an evidential psychic medium, which is one who provides facts and information that may be known only to the sitter (the one having the reading). She was described by her clients as "a warm and forthright medium."

Sandra appeared in the Netflix docuseries *Surviving Death*, which was directed by Ricki Stern and Jesse Sweet and based on the book *Surviving Death: A Journalist Investigates Evidence for an Afterlife* by Leslie Kean.

Sandra O'Hara passed away unexpectedly on September 2, 2021.

Permissions / Bibliography

"3 Reasons Why You Are Seeing 2:22: The Meaning of 222." November 11, 2020. Angel Number Meanings. WILLOW SOUL Heals. WillowSoul.com. Online: https://willowsoul.com/blogs/numbers/3-reasons-why-you-are-seeing-222-the-meaning-of-222.

"5 Reasons Why You Are Seeing 11:11: The Meaning of 1111." November 11, 2020. Angel Number Meanings. WILLOW SOUL Heals. WillowSoul.com. Online: https://willowsoul.com/blogs/numbers/5-reasons-why-you-are-seeing-11-11-the-meaning-of-1111.

"6 Reasons Why You Are Seeing 4:44: The Meaning of 444." November 11, 2020. Angel Number Meanings. WILLOW SOUL Heals. WillowSoul.com. Online: https://willowsoul.com/blogs/numbers/5-reasons-why-you-are-seeing-4-44-the-meaning-of-444.

"8 Reasons Why You Are Seeing 5:55: The Meaning of 555." November 11, 2020. Angel Number Meanings. WILLOW SOUL Heals. WillowSoul.com. Online: https://willowsoul.com/blogs/numbers/4-reasons-why-you-are-seeing-555-the-meaning-of-555.

Andrews, Lynn V. *The Power Deck: The Cards of Wisdom*. Beyond Words, 2019.

AFTERGLOW

Words and Music by Taylor Swift, Louis Bell, Adam King Feeney and Matthew Tavares
Copyright © 2019 SONGS OF UNIVERSAL, INC., TAYLOR SWIFT MUSIC, EMI APRIL MUSIC INC.,
QUIET AS KEPT MUSIC INC. and THIRD SIDE MUSIC INC.
All Rights for TAYLOR SWIFT MUSIC Administered by SONGS OF UNIVERSAL, INC.
All Rights for EMI APRIL MUSIC INC. and QUIET AS KEPT MUSIC INC. Administered by SONY MUSIC
PUBLISHING (US) LLC, 424 Church Street, Suite 1200, Nashville, TN 37219
All Rights Reserved Used by Permission
Reprinted by Permission of Hal Leonard LLC

ALL WE ARE

Words and Music by Matt Nathanson and Marshall Altman
Copyright © 2007 Stage Three Songs, Little Victories Music and MarshallAltmanMusic
All Rights for Stage Three Songs and Little Victories Music Administered by Stage Three Music (US) Inc., a BMG Rights Management (US) LLC company
All Rights for MarshallAltmanMusic Administered by Me Gusta Music
All Rights Reserved Used by Permission
Reprinted by Permission of Hal Leonard LLC

BE HERE NOW

Words and Music by Ray LaMontagne
Copyright © 2006 Sweet Mary Music
All Rights Administered by Hipgnosis Songs Group
All Rights Reserved Used by Permission
Reprinted by Permission of Hal Leonard LLC

DARLING

Words and Music by Ashley Frangipane, John Cunningham, Trent Reznor and Atticus Ross
Copyright © 2021 SONGS OF UNIVERSAL, INC., 17 BLACK MUSIC, RICTED, CUNNINGHAMBURGER
MUSIC, CLOUDCOVER, INC. and SONGS IN THE KEY OF MINK
All Rights for 17 BLACK MUSIC Administered by SONGS OF UNIVERSAL, INC.
All Rights for RICTED, CUNNINGHAMBURGER MUSIC and CLOUDCOVER INC. Administered
Worldwide by SONGS OF KOBALT MUSIC PUBLISHING
All Rights for SONGS IN THE KEY OF MINK Administered by DOWNTOWN DMP SONGS
All Rights Reserved Used by Permission
Reprinted by Permission of Hal Leonard LLC

EVERGREEN (Love Theme from "A Star is Born")

Words by PAUL WILLIAMS Music by BARBRA STREISAND
© 1976 (Renewed) WARNER-OLIVE MUSIC, LLC (ASCAP)
All Rights (Excluding Print) for WARNER-OLIVE MUSIC, LLC (ASCAP) and Administered by UNIVERSAL MUSIC CORP. (ASCAP)
Exclusive Worldwide Print Rights Administered by ALFRED MUSIC
All Rights Reserved
Used by Permission of ALFRED MUSIC

EVERYTHING I OWN

Words and Music by David Gates
Copyright © 1972 Sony Music Publishing (US) LLC
Copyright Renewed
All Rights Administered by Sony Music Publishing (US) LLC, 424 Church Street, Suite 1200, Nashville, TN 37219
International Copyright Secured All Rights Reserved
Reprinted by Permission of Hal Leonard LLC

INCOMPLETE

Words and Music by CHRIS LEONARD, JAKE GOSLING and JAMES BAY
© 2016 WARNER/CHAPPELL MUSIC PUBLISHING LTD, BDI MUSIC LIMITED and B UNIQUE MUSIC LIMITED
All Rights for WARNER/CHAPPELL MUSIC PUBLISHING LTD in the U.S. and Canada Administered by WB MUSIC CORP.
All Rights Reserved
Used by Permission of ALFRED MUSIC

INCOMPLETE

Words and Music by James Bay, Chris Leonard and Jake Gosling
Copyright © 2014 Concord Copyrights Aldwych Ltd., Warner Chappell Music Publishing Ltd. and BDI Music Limited
All Rights for Concord Copyrights Aldwych Ltd. Administered by Concord Copyrights c/o Concord Music Publishing
All Rights for Warner Chappell Music Publishing Ltd. Administered by WC Music Corp.
All Rights Reserved Used by Permission
Reprinted by Permission of Hal Leonard LLC
Reprinted by Permission of The Royalty Network, Inc.

JUST BREATHE

Words and Music by Eddie Vedder
Copyright © 2009 INNOCENT BYSTANDER
All Rights administered by UNIVERSAL MUSIC WORKS
All Rights Reserved. Used by Permission.
Reprinted by Permission of Hal Leonard LLC

ONE MORE KISS, DEAR

Words by PETER SKELLERN, Music by EVANGELOS PAPA-THANASSIOU
© 1994 MUFTI MUSIC LTD (NS)
All Rights on Behalf of MUFTI MUSIC LTD Administered by WC MUSIC CORP.
All Rights Reserved
Used by Permission of ALFRED MUSIC

ONE MORE KISS, DEAR

Words by Peter Skellern
Music by Evanghelos Papathanassiou
Copyright © 1994 WARNER-BARHAM MUSIC LLC and MUFTI MUSIC LTD
All Rights for WARNER-BARHAM MUSIC LLC Administered by SONGS OF UNIVERSAL, INC.
All Rights for MUFTI MUSIC LTD Administered by WC MUSIC CORP.
All Rights Reserved Used by Permission
Reprinted by Permission of Hal Leonard LLC

THIS AIN'T GOODBYE

Words and Music by Pat Monahan and Ryan Tedder
Copyright © 2009 EMI April Music Inc., Blue Lamp Music and Write 2 Live Publishing
All Rights on behalf of EMI April Music Inc. and Blue Lamp Music Administered by Sony Music Publishing (US) LLC, 424 Church Street, Suite 1200, Nashville, TN 37219
All Rights on behalf of Write 2 Live Publishing Administered by Concord Avenue c/o Concord Music Publishing
International Copyright Secured All Rights Reserved
Reprinted by Permission of Hal Leonard LLC

REVIEW ASK

Urgent Plea!

Thank you for purchasing a copy of *Faith, Hope & Love, A Survivor's Memoir*. I am honored you took the time to open your heart and soul to my journey of grieving. I would love to hear from you if this story has helped you process your grief.

Please take a moment to post a review on Amazon. Your feedback and support are greatly appreciated.

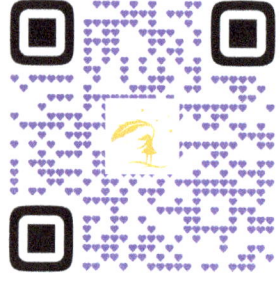

Scan To Review

www.ingramcontent.com/pod-product-compliance
Lightning Source LLC
Chambersburg PA
CBHW051620010526
44119CB00009B/222